Tom Elliott's work offers us a path to wholehearted living, showing us, through the time-tested wisdom of St. Ignatius Loyola, how to live with passion, focus, and conviction. I recommend this book for anyone who wants to dive into the deep of life rather than wading near life's surface, who desires to live wholly rather than fragmentarily, purposefully rather than just getting along. This book is funny, poignant, and profound—the real deal—the kind of book that can really change your life. • **Stephen J. Binz,** *biblical scholar, speaker, and author of* ***Threshold Bible Study***

Drawing on his twenty years of experience as a spiritual director, Tom Elliott has become a valued voice on Ignatian spirituality. His first book, *The Intimacy You Desire*, offers a wonderful overview of the *Spiritual Exercises*, while his second book, *Becoming Wholehearted*, dives into the invitation to wholeness and holiness in the *Exercises*. Elliott offers meaningful examples of this invitation in each chapter. Even those who are already familiar with the *Exercises* will be surprised by the new approach Elliott offers to the meditations in Week Two. • **James Martin, SJ,** *author of* ***Learning to Pray*** *and* ***Building a Bridge***

Tom Elliott provides a useful guide to restoring energy and meaning when discouragement tempts us to resign ourselves to a life of dissatisfaction and compromise. Offering practical ways to "reboot" when we feel stuck and weary, his suggestions are rooted in the classical wisdom of St. Ignatius' *Spiritual Exercises*, sensitively adapted to the struggles of people today. Replete with rich illustrations from his personal life and work with others, this book reflects Elliott's insightfulness and compassion as a caring pastoral minister. • **Wilkie Au, PhD,** *co-author of* ***God's Unconditional Love: Healing Our Shame***

Tom invites readers to accompany him into his own real and deep journey into wholeheartedness as they reflect on their own. His great honesty about his own struggles and joys, desolations and consolations will help readers to be courageous, honest, and real with God as they enter into the *Spiritual Exercises*. This book offers many examples of individuals struggling to live a wholehearted life with and in Jesus. Readers will discover that the *Exercises* are about us as well as Jesus Christ; they are about letting Jesus companion with us in our life experiences as well as being Jesus' companion in his life. • **Maureen Conroy, RSM, DMin,** *author of* ***Looking into the Well*** *and* ***The Discerning Heart***

I used *Becoming Wholehearted* as a guide for my own personal annual retreat, and it led me to deep and fresh experiences of meditations I've been praying with my whole adult life. I can think of no higher praise for a book than to say that it led me closer to Christ, and Tom's book did this for me. • **Mark E. Thibodeaux, SJ,** *author of* ***Armchair Mystic***

Becoming Wholehearted

Growing in Authentic Passion through the Spiritual Exercises of Saint Ignatius

Tom Elliott

twentythirdpublications.com

Twenty-Third Publications
One Montauk Avenue
New London, CT 06320
(860) 437-3012 or (800) 321-0411
www.twentythirdpublications.com

Copyright © 2021 Tom Elliott. All rights reserved. No part of this publication may be reproduced in any manner without prior written permission of the publisher. Write to the Permissions Editor.

Cover photo: Fr. Lawrence Lew, OP

ISBN: 978-1-62785-636-2
Printed in the U.S.A.

A division of Bayard, Inc.

Dedication and Gratitude

I dedicate this book to my wife, Carmel, who makes God's unconditional love and acceptance tangible to me every day and inspires me to become more wholehearted, and to my parents and siblings, who have supported me in every way and during every season of life.

I am grateful for all of the men and women who allow me to companion with them in spiritual direction and supervision. Their faith and life stories inspire me to be a better man. I am also grateful for Morgan Ford Rice at Red Oar Writing for not only editing my books, but also being a source of encouragement and challenge. Not least of all, I'm grateful for Twenty-Third Publications for their continued support of my writing and for their excellence and dedication to bringing readers meaningful spiritual material.

Contents

1 **INTRODUCTION**
Into the Deep

12 **CHAPTER ONE**
The Wholeheartedness of Companionship
The Kingdom Exercise

34 **CHAPTER TWO**
Wholeheartedness in the Beginning
The Infancy Narratives

52 **CHAPTER THREE**
Wholeheartedness through Compassion
The Two Standards

68 **CHAPTER FOUR**
Wholeheartedness through *Magis*
The Three Types of Persons

86 **CHAPTER FIVE**
Wholeheartedness through Opposition
The Three Degrees of Humility

106 **CHAPTER SIX**
Examples of Wholeheartedness

115 **CONCLUSION**

INTRODUCTION

Into the Deep

Some people consider me a failure because, sixteen years after ordination, I left the priesthood. To be honest, there are days I wake up agreeing with them. I'm not a person who flippantly makes commitments and then backs out of them. In fact, I've always prided myself on not only finishing a job but also finishing it perfectly. That pursuit of perfection began very early in my life. As a child, I connected being perfect with being loved. By the time I was a teenager, my desire to serve and my need to feel perfect were already directing my life toward seminary. It was only after eight years of seminary and many years of priesthood that I realized being an ordained perfectionist did not lead me to wholehearted living and the joy of passionate service, but rather, to a very dark place where I felt like I was living other people's expectations rather than my heart's most authentic desires.

The dark and oppressive grip of perfectionism began loosening when I learned about Ignatius of Loyola, a sixteenth-century saint from Spain. Despite having lived five hundred years ago, his experiences, meditations, and wisdom have profoundly shaped my life. While many people might view him as a larger-than-life figure from a time when knights in shining armor rescued damsels in distress, I have come to see Ignatius as a true friend who, through his writing, vulnerably shares his struggles and successes in ways that help me to be more wholehearted. I'm sure you can think of people like that in your life—men and women who became extraordinary mentors, companions, and sources of encouragement for you. Such people are tremendous gifts to us and are necessary guides into the wholeheartedness we desire.

I was introduced to Ignatius when I enrolled in spiritual direction training a few years after ordination. My classmates and I spent three years studying his famous retreat manual, the *Spiritual Exercises*, which Ignatius worked on from 1521 until he died in 1556. I'd love to say that by the time I was certified in spiritual direction I completely understood the *Exercises*, but that would be a lie. In fact, I barely understood the meditations and prayers in the *Exercises* in my head, let alone my heart. It wasn't until a few years after my certification in spiritual direction that my director prayerfully guided me through Ignatius' retreat manual over the course of more than four years. During that time, the wisdom and transformative power of the *Exercises* moved from my head to my heart.

During those four years, the one to two hours I spent every day using Ignatius' *Exercises* in personal prayer were life-changing. I learned for the first time that discerning God's will is rooted in acknowledging our heart's most genuine desires, which is much different from trying to satisfy the perceived expectations of God and others, which is what I was raised to believe. I also learned that Ignatius strongly cautioned anyone who was considering changing a major decision or vocation. Since by that point I had begun re-discerning my priesthood, I responded to Ignatius' caution by finding a therapist who was willing to join my spiritual director in accompanying me on the journey.

By the time I finished all of the meditations in the retreat manual, I not only experienced an intimacy with God that I could never have fathomed, but I also felt for the first time the freedom to ask some hard questions about my perfectionism and my priesthood, and to be open to new answers and paths. The honesty and vulnerability I learned in my relationship with God through the *Exercises* began manifesting in other relationships as well, which confirmed for me that I didn't have to be perfect in order to be loved.

While it's a rarity that the freedom people experience through the prayers and meditations in Ignatius' *Exercises* leads them to amend a major decision in their lives, it did for me, and within a year of finishing, I left the priesthood and started serving full-time as a spiritual director. As you might imagine, those months of transition were marked with moments of great hope and peace, as well as questioning and suffering. Through it all, my spiritual director continued encouraging me to be honest with myself and with God regarding my deepest and most authentic desires. As months turned into years, I found myself more and more grateful for the freedom and vulnerability God and Ignatius taught me through the *Exercises*.

Finally feeling settled personally, spiritually, and professionally, I decided to go through the *Exercises* again at my own pace, but with a different focus. Rather than discerning my heart's most authentic desires, I longed for the very same thing you do—practical spiritual help for living a wholehearted life—a life marked by authentic passion, generosity, willingness, availability, and selflessness. I desired more than simply feeling like I was on the right path; I desired to intentionally and wholeheartedly walk that path in a way that allowed God to transform me into the image and likeness of Christ I was created to be, and in a way that helped others to encounter God. As I continually took that desire to God in prayer, he showed me two important things.

The first thing God helped me to see was that wholeheartedness is primarily about going deeper. Just as a submarine can move horizontally, from one sea to another, and move vertically to various depths, God revealed to me that life is made up of two primary movements.

Like a submarine trying to find the correct "sea," some of the decisions you and I face in life belong to the horizontal plane—they are choices about "which"—which vocation, which relationships, which job, which ministry, etc. Such decisions have to do with the *circumstances* and *relationships* of life. Those are the decisions that Ignatius originally intended to help people discern through the *Exercises* retreat.

Once the submarine of our lives moves to the place we most authentically desire to be on that horizontal plane, or where the circumstances of life take us, then we are given new opportunities to move on the vertical plane, into the deep. Rather than our decisions focusing on "which," they become more about "how"—how willing, how magnanimous, how passionate, how wholehearted will we live in each particular circumstance?

The image of the submarine, which I used often in prayer, was very important to me and helped me realize that my first time through the *Exercises* helped me navigate to the "sea" of my heart's deepest desires. My hope for the second time through the *Exercises* was to dive deeper. However, I knew that in order to go deeper, I needed to better understand what that vertical, deeper, more passionate choice meant. What would it mean in my life if I let my heart become like a diving submarine, moving into the deep?

I didn't realize the profound relevancy of the submarine image until I read Richard Rohr's book *Falling Upward*, and Ronald Rolheiser's book *Sacred Fire*. Those two books helped me better understand the submarine's two movements. Rather than using the language of "horizontal plane" and "vertical plane," Rohr uses "first half of life" and "second half of life," and Rolheiser uses "getting our lives together" and "giving our lives away." Regardless of the imagery or phrasing, it's clear that life doesn't end when we feel settled (or stuck) spiritually, emotionally, professionally, or vocationally in a particular space. Instead, there is a new and deeper movement available to us. That is the movement you and I desire. We desire to passionately and wholeheartedly move into the deep—into greater generosity, willingness, and availability—in the various circumstances in our lives.

Sadly, there are very few people courageous enough to move into the deep. It feels safer to stay on the surface where our lives are primarily directed by our egos and we can protect ourselves from much of the vulnerability and pain of life. This is the very reason why it's hard to find wisdom figures in our culture today. Not many people have made the deeper journey. Instead, many have all too often chosen to float on the surface of life, defensively promoting their own opinions and choices while demanding that others be like them and acquiesce to them. In that place of spiritual and emotional immaturity, their zeal is a profoundly false passion that brings about division, isolationism, and violence. While such false passion is rampant in our world today, hope is not lost. The fact that you're reading this book is a testament to that hope.

Unlike the false passion and hard-heartedness that makes the news every day, there are people like us who desire authentic passion and wholeheartedness. That desire manifests itself in peace, connectedness, and service. It reveals itself to the world through our trust that God is present in every circumstance and that meaning can be found everywhere and in everyone. As such, we intentionally try to choose in each moment of our lives that which is most loving, generous, magnanimous, selfless, and hopeful. Courageously pushing past our fear of being hurt, we decide to be vulnerable with God and others. As we go deeper, we find that our capacity to be accepting, merciful, and gentle expands exponentially. We are spiritual submarines who don't want to end the journey on the surface; rather, we desire to move into the deep.

The great poet T.S. Eliot confirms that people like us exist. He believed that, while some people become apathetic, resentful, and withdrawn in the circumstances of their lives, there are those who daringly choose to go deeper. At the end of his poem "East Coker," in the *Four Quartets,* Eliot puts eloquent words to my lumbering image of the submarine, writing, "Love is most nearly itself when here and now ceases to matter." In other words, our most wholehearted living isn't based on the "here and now"—the circumstances of our lives—but rather, on something deeper. In case we missed that point, Eliot continues explaining,

> Old men ought to be explorers
> Here and there does not matter
> We must be still and still moving
> Into another intensity
> For a further union, a deeper communion

What powerful words! At the very times in our lives when some would say we should, at best, just find a way to minimally get by, or at worse, just wait to die, some people choose to be explorers. That is precisely what you and I desire. We desire to be still in the circumstances of our lives while moving deeper into greater passion and wholeheartedness, into a further union with ourselves, others, and creation, and into a deeper communion with Christ. How do we make this further journey into the deep? As I began the *Exercises* again, God answered that question by showing me a second thing—the part of Ignatius' retreat manual known as Week Two.

If you're not familiar with the *Exercises*, you're probably asking, "What is Week Two?" Simply put, it's the second part of the retreat. You see, Ignatius wrote the *Exercises* so that they could be used for a 30-day silent retreat. Since the prayers and meditations were structured for a month-long retreat, Ignatius referred to the four sections of the manual as "Weeks." For each of the Four Weeks, Ignatius challenges retreatants to focus on a particular spiritual gift, known as a grace. The first part of the *Exercises,* Week One, encourages us to pray for the grace to experience and accept that we are loved sinners, cherished by God beyond imagining. In Week Two, Ignatius invites us to know Christ more intimately and companion with him more closely. Then, in the third section of the retreat, Week Three, we use the passion narratives in the four gospels as we pray for the grace to be with Christ in his suffering. The *Exercises* end with Week Four, during which time we enter into the joy of Christ's resurrection.

While Ignatius invites us to focus on a very specific spiritual gift during each of the Four Weeks of the *Exercises,* he also gives permission to spiritual directors to adapt the prayers and meditations in ways that can benefit retreatants and better fit their schedule. I did just that as God drew my attention back to Week Two; I began using the same meditations and prayers that had years earlier helped me to discern God's will and that had challenged me to know Christ more intimately and companion with him more closely, and I let them lead me into the deep. As I did, I discovered that the meditations in Week Two can be used not only to discern an important decision, but they can also be used to learn the five common sources of apathy and half-heartedness in our lives and help to deepen wholeheartedness and rekindle our life's passion in five prayerful and practical ways.

That discovery was really important for me because the more I read books about wholehearted living, such as *The Gifts of Imperfection* by Brené Brown and *Uninvited* by Lysa TerKeurst, I realized that they all stopped short of offering practical spiritual tools and meditations. I needed and wanted more than simply acknowledging the areas of my life where half-heartedness and apathy penetrate; I wanted to encounter Christ in the intimacy of personal prayer and be led by him to a pervasive authenticity and generosity.

As I spent time in prayer with Ignatius' meditations from Week Two, focusing on the grace of wholeheartedness, I discovered some of the spiritual fruit frequently associated with passionate and wholehearted living, like joy, generosity, and selflessness. That led me to share what I was learning with some of my directees, most of whom also experienced renewed and deepened wholeheartedness. Encouraged by their feedback, I offered several retreats throughout the world, presenting the material in this book and noting how people responded to it. The affirmations I received from directees and retreatants helped me to realize that, while there is no quick and easy way to stay passionate and wholehearted, the lessons and meditations in Week Two can significantly help. They give us the practical spiritual tools we need to dive deeper.

Of course, the spiritual tools we find in Week Two are by no means easy shortcuts. In fact, if you're looking for a quick fix to half-heartedness and apathy in your life, then this book is not for you. However, if you're interested in spiritual resources rooted in the Christian tradition that can draw you deeper into passionate and wholehearted living through prayer and reflection, then this book will help.

Before continuing to the next chapter, I encourage you to take a moment to acknowledge to God which particular circumstance in your life currently leaves you feeling the deepest desolation, emptiness, fatigue, and apathy. Maybe you're feeling lonely in your marriage, burned out at work, debilitated by health issues, exhausted as a caregiver, or ineffective in ministry. Are you able to describe how you're feeling right now about that particular area of your life? Is there any specific aspect of that circumstance that causes the most desolation?

Regardless of what area of your life is currently marked with the darkness of desolation, there is hope. In the upcoming chapters, you will learn about and reflect on five specific spiritual tools for rekindling passion and wholeheartedness. Whether you're feeling lonely and disconnected, unsettled and lost, victimized and powerless, exhausted and complacent, or irrelevant and discouraged, it is my sincere hope that many of the stories, experiences, meditations, and reflection questions in this book will help you. I encourage you to frequently return to the parts of this book that you find the most meaningful. As spiritual companions, let's head into the deep together, trusting that God desires our passionate wholeheartedness even more than we do.

CHAPTER ONE

The Wholeheartedness of Companionship

The Kingdom Exercise

Some people's lives begin with tragedy and challenges. That is how Ignatius' life began. Shortly after his birth in 1491, his mother died. Loss and disconnection continued for the child as his father entrusted him to a local blacksmith's young wife, Maria, to nurse him. Even though their house was only a half-mile from the Loyola family castle, Ignatius was brought up markedly disconnected from his own family. Such experiences of loss can leave us feeling desolate and lonely, and Ignatius' life was riddled with such experiences.

By the age of sixteen, Ignatius had lost his father and one of his six older brothers. While it would be expected that those losses would bring about moments of great loneliness, it's quite possible that the darkest desolation was the loss of Ignatius' hope for glory, which a cannonball shattered when Ignatius was about thirty years old. Like so many young men of his generation, Ignatius hoped and fantasized about winning glory, fame, and women through his service as a soldier in the Spanish army. Yet, those hopes were crushed when a cannonball struck him in the leg during the battle at Pamplona.

Ignatius' recovery at the family castle was long and painful. He spent a lot of time alone, undoubtedly grieving the loss of his ambitions. In order to pass the time, he asked for some books; reading was one of his favorite pastimes. The castle, however, did not have any of the romance novels that Ignatius preferred, but only a copy of the lives of the saints and a book on the life of Christ. As he read those books, an important transformation and conversion began. Ignatius found himself connecting more and more deeply with the stories of the saints and Christ, to the point of experiencing companionship with them.

While he was often disconnected from others in the physical sense, he was growing in ever deeper companionship with the Trinity and the saints in the spiritual sense. His personal prayer moved from merely rote offerings to casual conversations with saints and members of the Trinity that Ignatius called colloquies. Those deep spiritual friendships rekindled Ignatius' wholeheartedness, but instead of being passionate about military service, he became passionate about serving God and others.

Like Saint Ignatius, you and I have experienced the desolation and apathy that come with feeling lonely and disconnected. My own loneliness and disconnection did not come from loss, but rather from fear. I spent most of my life fearing that, if I let others get too close to me, they would find out that I'm not good enough. I didn't come to that awareness until I was in my 30s, but there were signs of it much earlier in my life. For example, I remember being a senior in high school and my girlfriend and I were making out in the car before class and she whispered, "I love you," and all I could squeak out was, "Uh-huh." The look on her face indicated that my reply did not meet her expectation. I justified my response, thinking, "The words, 'I love you,' are *too important* to casually throw around!" I can see now that, in actuality, I was just afraid of saying those words; I was afraid of any intimate companionship that might lead to being rejected by others.

As you can imagine, celibate priesthood was a pretty safe place for me to fearfully hide from intimate companionship. Yet, despite the many layers of emotional protection that priesthood provided, God still found a way to challenge me to face my fear of intimate companionship, including through a sweet, elderly lady named Nancy, who sat in the back pew at Christ the King Catholic Church every Saturday evening.

Christ the King was my longest pastorate, lasting seven years. Just a year before being transferred there, I had finally learned how to spend time with God in personal prayer. I was enjoying praying about an hour each day and changes were happening within me. I can look back now and see that my commitment to personal prayer was slowly leading me to a new and deeper acceptance of love and companionship. As I settled into my new assignment at Christ the King, God chose Nancy to be the catalyst for healing my fear of intimate companionship.

The vigil Mass at Christ the King was at 6 pm with confessions beginning at 5 pm. Each Saturday, as I walked through the back of church from the confessional to the sacristy to prepare for the liturgy, Nancy would hear me passing by and call to me. Even though she was legally blind, she somehow knew that it was I walking behind her. As I stopped and knelt beside her, she would whisper, "I love you, Fr. Tom." Despite how embarrassing it is for me to admit this, my response each week to Nancy's kind words was, "Uh-huh." I hated that response! It was a weekly reminder of my fear of intimate companionship! I found that more and more of my personal prayer time was consumed with sharing with God my frustrations about love and companionship.

Thankfully, after months of prayerful struggle, and months of answering, "Uh-huh," I was finally able to change my response and say to Nancy, "I love you, too." That response broke an emotional logjam in my heart and I found that love, companionship, vulnerability, and intimacy began moving through me like the Mississippi River, with strength and determination. I was able to be more present with people, not just physically near them, but more emotionally and spiritually *with* them. I doubt most people even noticed this change in me because I had become very adept at faking companionship and intimacy with people, but God and I noticed, and maybe Nancy did too.

Having companioned with hundreds of men and women as a spiritual director, I can confidently say that the fear of not being good enough is the *primary fear* that every single one of us carries deep in our hearts. It's the wound that we struggle with most of our lives and, hopefully, it's a lie that is eventually healed through the truth that we are, in fact, good enough for companionship and vulnerable intimacy; we are good enough for others and for God. Coming to that realization, however, is not easy for most of us. In fact, we tend to be very creative about how we hide from that fear and wound. I, like many, hid in isolation and loneliness. I know that doesn't sound very pleasant, but there is an undeniable emotional safety in loneliness. And the aloneness and loneliness of priesthood seemed particularly safe.

Regardless of what caused our loneliness and disconnection, we know that they are very empty and dark places. They're desolate because they're contrary to how we were created. We were born out of the vulnerable intimacy of the Trinity and were created to live in companionship with God, others, and all of creation. Therefore, when the circumstances of our lives or the choices we make disconnect us from our companionship with God and others, it leaves us apathetic and desolate. Being disconnected from God and others keeps us from the wholeheartedness we desire. Ignatius clearly understood that truth and chose to cultivate the passion that comes from companionship. Maybe that's why he wrote the *Spiritual Exercises* with a profound emphasis on deepening our intimacy with God, ourselves, others, and all of creation. He knew that we were created for companionship and that such vulnerable intimacy would set our hearts on fire to live magnanimous lives of love.

Regardless of whether we choose to companion with someone, or they choose to companion with us, that loving connection can enflame and expand our heart, drawing us into courage and wholeheartedness. As such, companionship can be the very thing that inspires a husband to give up smoking, motivates a wife to attend Alcoholics Anonymous, moves a teacher to stay after school to help a student, increases a pastor's patience with his congregation, and deepens a parent's generosity toward her child. Not only is that truth confirmed by our experiences, but it is also confirmed by research, including five studies done in 2014 at Stanford University and a study at Yale in 2018. The results of those experiments show that when we have a sense of working with others it increases our participation and can even transform how we view challenges and struggles. For example, what seemed like difficult work when we thought we were alone can become playful and enjoyable when we believe that we're with others. Since life is frequently filled with difficult work and circumstances, intimate companionship must be a constant in order for us to remain wholehearted.

One of the first times I experienced how companionship can realistically lead to greater joy, passion, and willingness was when my sister, Vikki, asked me to help her move. A few years after Vikki got married, she and her husband relocated to Tulsa, Oklahoma. They asked me to help them move into their new apartment, which was on the third floor of a large building complex on 71st Street. As I pulled into the parking lot and assessed the situation, I realized that their question, "Would you mind helping us move this weekend?" was actually camouflaging the real question, "Will you risk your life hauling a full-sized sleeper sofa up two flights of stairs that contain four ridiculously narrow 180-degree turns?"

Very few people in their right mind would willingly choose to help someone move a sleeper sofa up two flights of stairs, yet I did. Why? It's because I love my sister and brother-in-law and desire to be a part of their lives. My desire to companion with them filled me with willingness and joy, despite facing the nearly impossible mission of wrangling the cumbersome sofa up the stairwell gauntlet. Years later, as I reflected on that experience, I began to realize in a tangible way that human companionship is a powerful source of wholeheartedness, especially in circumstances where we would not have otherwise chosen to be generous and willing.

While Nancy and Vikki helped me to see more clearly how human companionship can infuse our lives with wholeheartedness and lead us to a place we would not have otherwise gone, God still needed to show me how *Christ's* companionship could also enflame my passion and magnanimity. That's very important because, let's face it, there are times in our lives when we don't have, or we *feel* like we don't have, the companionship of anyone other than God. Thankfully, years after the sleeper sofa had ascended to its new home, and a year after being assigned as the administrator of a Catholic school, God taught me that lesson.

I was assigned to a school that had been struggling for a few years. People within the school who should have had the authority to make positive changes felt undercut and disempowered by those who should not have been making decisions. That tension frequently spilled over into our school board meetings, drenching them in frustration. The school felt like a sinking ship, and I didn't want to be the captain when it went under. As my time was more and more consumed with the administrative details of the school, I felt increasingly detached from Christ. I knew I needed to bring those feelings into the light of spiritual direction.

Walking into my spiritual director's office, I flopped onto a large, cushioned chair across from him and vented about my fatigue in dealing with one particularly egotistical person at the school. After listening to my explanation as to why I was going to ask the bishop to relieve me of my assignment at the school, my director gently asked, "Where is Jesus during the school board meetings?" The question triggered a loud scoff from me and I blurted out, "Jesus doesn't want to have a damn thing to do with those meetings!" I knew that wasn't true, but it felt good saying it. I'm sure I unconsciously hoped my childish response would cause my spiritual director to say something like, "Well, Tom, I agree. There are some wounded people associated with that school and you need to be transferred to a place that is running smoothly and can appreciate your ability to keep things running that way." Of course, that's not how he responded.

The rest of the spiritual direction session was challenging. My director invited me to prayerfully imagine being at one of those school board meetings, focused on Jesus' presence, words, and actions. Through the experience, I came to realize that Jesus was not only present, but he was also grateful for *my* presence. Jesus needed me to be at those meetings, bringing his encouragement, hope, healing, and love to the school. I was not alone, and neither was Christ.

Thankfully, my director helped me understand that my own ego was the largest in the board meetings. That awareness continued to deepen within me and, in the months that followed, I noticed that when I focused on the divisions and egos involved at the school, as well as my own fears and wounds, I felt half-hearted, passionless, and apathetic; whereas, when I focused on Christ's companionship with me in that ministry, I felt willing and magnanimous. It was a life-changing lesson.

How is Christ's companionship helping rekindle your life's passion, especially in that particular circumstance that has become dark and difficult? If you're like most people, you haven't yet asked or answered that question. While it's easy to note which family members and friends are with us in particular circumstances, reflecting on Christ's companionship can seem a bit daunting. Thankfully, one of Ignatius' meditations in Week Two of the *Spiritual Exercises*, known as the Kingdom Exercise, can help. It was written specifically to impassion us through companionship with Christ. Before we apply the meditation to your circumstance, let's take a brief look at it and how it helped a faith-filled woman named Madeline.

On the surface, the Kingdom Exercise seems pretty mundane, maybe even boring. Drawing on imagery that was common in the sixteenth century, Ignatius invites us to prayerfully imagine that a wonderful Christian king invites us to be a part of a mission. The king desires for us to journey with him, eating what he eats and sleeping where he sleeps. That sounds pretty boring, right? Well, here's where things get interesting—the Kingdom Exercise is not meant to be theoretical, but rather, personal. In other words, we are invited to reflect on what our heartfelt response would be to a person whom we greatly admire choosing us as an intimate companion. Has someone whom you deeply admire ever chosen you for something special? Think about that for a moment. If that has happened, then you know the wholehearted response Ignatius is inviting us to experience in this meditation.

As the meditation continues, the focus is clearly on companionship—eating what the king eats, drinking what he drinks, and wearing what he wears—and not on what he wants us to achieve. In fact, nowhere in the meditation are we told what specific assignment the king wants us to accomplish. The focus is simply on how much we admire the king, and the gratitude, honor, and willingness we feel at the opportunity to be with him. Ignatius then invites us to acknowledge those feelings and apply them to the second part of the meditation—our companionship with Christ.

If our hearts are filled with honor, humility, and gratitude at being asked by an earthly king to journey with him, how much more will we be inspired by the Eternal King's invitation? Ignatius invites us to spend time prayerfully imagining Jesus inviting us to companion with him on a special mission. As we reflect on what it is like to be so close to Christ, participating in a mission with him, we will undoubtedly feel a specific response welling up within us. Such meaningful companionship will most likely cause us to want to be more conscious of who Christ is for us and to wholeheartedly respond to his presence and love.

Our reaction to being invited to companion with Christ will naturally lead most of us to profess and demonstrate our commitment to him in a way that is similar to Ruth's commitment to her mother-in-law, Naomi, when she told her, "Wherever you go I will go, wherever you lodge I will lodge. Your people shall be my people and your God, my God. Where you die I will die, and there be buried" (Ruth 1:16–17a). Such an expression of commitment to companionship is the third and last part of the Kingdom Exercise, a part I like to call the "prayer of intention."

In his book *Draw Me Into Your Friendship,* David Fleming offers a beautiful paraphrase of Ignatius' sample prayer of intention, writing,

> Eternal Lord and King of all creation, humbly I come before you. Knowing the support of Mary, your mother, and all your saints, I am moved by your grace to offer myself to you and to your work. I deeply desire to be with you in accepting all wrongs and rejections and all poverty, both actual and spiritual—and deliberately choose this, if it is for your greater service and praise. If you, my Lord and King, would so call and choose me, then take and receive me into such a way of life.

While that prayer is beautiful, it cannot possibly capture and express the uniqueness of each individual's wholehearted response to Christ's invitation into companionship. Instead, our response must be much more personal. In fact, if we really want to shift our focus from the details of our circumstances, which often suck the life out of us, causing deep loneliness, and enter more deeply into wholeheartedness through an awareness of our companionship with Christ, then we have to let go of the trappings of sixteenth-century kingship and let this meditation become very personal. That's what I encouraged Madeline to do when she came to me for spiritual direction.

Seventeen years after their wedding, Madeline and her husband were living separate lives but under one roof. It wasn't a sudden or traumatic event that caused their apathy but the monotonous, slow ticking of ordinary events of life. The passionate tides of romance they experienced the first few years of their marriage had ebbed, leaving a barrenness that now, sadly, felt normal. They no longer enjoyed physical intimacy, rarely communicated about anything other than their schedules and responsibilities, and busied themselves with work. The little energy they possessed was spent on their two children. During a spiritual direction session, Madeline summarized her emotional and spiritual mood, saying to me, "I'm lonely and tired. Something has to change because I am not going to keep living this way."

Madeline had already spent time and energy trying to renew her marriage. She had wisely consulted a physician about her symptoms of depression. She had also sought the help of a therapist. It was clear to me that she was not taking her loneliness and fatigue lightly and did not view divorce as a quick fix. She was spiritually mature enough to know that her deepest desire was a renewed and healthy disposition toward her husband rather than running from the pain of her circumstance. Her maturity was demonstrated in the fervent prayers for patience and strength she offered to God during those dark times of loneliness and exhaustion.

Many of us can empathize with Madeline. At various times throughout our lives, in our vocations or in important decisions, we've become over-focused on the details and responsibilities and felt a similar loneliness and fatigue. When those feelings become pervasive and dark, they can break something deep within us. Madeline had reached that point; she knew something needed to change. Thankfully, she wasn't naively hoping to eliminate all loneliness and fatigue from her life, but rather, she desired to rekindle her passion for her husband in a way that would bear good spiritual and emotional fruit for them and their children.

As we spent more time together, Madeline helped me to see that her focus throughout the day was rarely on Christ's presence in her circumstances, but rather on the countless unmet expectations that filled her daily routine. Like Saint Peter trying to walk on water, Madeline was easily distracted by the storms of life, manifested in countless daily details. For example, she explained to me that she and her husband had assigned one another specific chores each week and often they became resentful trying to figure out who wasn't doing enough. The bills were handled in a similar way; she and her husband were each responsible for paying different bills out of their separate accounts. Their emphasis on divvying up responsibilities often led to arguments. The more Madeline shared, the more it became clear that her focus was rarely on relationship, including Christ's companionship with her, but rather, it was on details and duties. She confirmed this when she shared with me the moment something broke deep within her.

It was Saturday morning, and Madeline and her husband were at the house with their kids. While the boys slept and her husband drank a cup of coffee on the couch, Madeline made breakfast and cleaned the kitchen. Working alone, she was overwhelmed with anger and felt unappreciated. When her husband walked into the room, she exploded with words of criticism. He stood there quietly staring at her as she talked down to him like a demanding boss to a disappointing employee. Madeline's powerful outburst scared her, and she realized that her relationship with her husband had become more like that of a supervisor to a worker—focused on details, tasks, and responsibilities. For the first time, she was aware that they no longer talked about *how* they were doing, but only about *what* they were doing.

Much like those moments when we isolate ourselves out of fear of intimacy, our hyper-focus on details, responsibilities, and deadlines can easily cause us to lose touch with Christ's presence in our lives, and we can find ourselves burned out, half-hearted, and lonely. The Kingdom Exercise offers us hope through a renewed focus on our companionship with Christ. Madeline clearly desired that spiritual renewal. As she began using the Kingdom Exercise during prayer each day, I encouraged her to make it as deeply personal and meaningful as possible. For Madeline, that meant prayerfully imagining that her favorite poet, Maya Angelou, invited her to be a part of a symposium on poetry.

It would not have moved Madeline's heart to begin the Kingdom Exercise imagining a sixteenth-century king inviting her on a mission. Therefore, Madeline made the meditation personal by tapping into her love for poetry. She imagined that Maya called and invited her to an amazing poetry conference where Madeline would not only get to hear some of her favorite poets, but she would also get to share some of her own poems. She explained to me that, as she imagined Maya's invitation, she felt humbled, accepted, appreciated, and valued. She also felt excited.

As the days unfolded, Madeline slowly moved to the second part of the Kingdom Exercise, shifting her focus from imagining companionship with Maya to reflecting on her companionship with Christ. Madeline imagined being invited by Christ to be part of the poetry symposium. She prayerfully paid attention to what Jesus looked like and what words he used to express his desire for her to accompany him to the conference. She was once again overwhelmed with gratitude and a sense of being appreciated and valued. She realized that the conference meant less to her than the time she would get to spend with Jesus. Madeline wanted to be near him and be aware of his reaction to her poetry. She desired for Jesus to be proud of her.

As Madeline spent more and more time with the Kingdom Exercise, she felt a rekindling happening and wanted it to influence every aspect of her life, not just an imaginary poetry conference. For example, she desired to be close to Christ and to be aware of his response to the love she showed her husband. She desired to give Jesus reasons to be proud of her. Madeline felt less alone and sensed a renewed willingness to be vulnerable with her husband. She let those feelings inspire a prayer of intention, which she slowly wrote in her prayer journal over the course of three days. When the prayer was finally finished, it was a beautiful expression of Madeline's desire to companion with Christ in every aspect of her life, especially the specific ways she hoped to serve Christ by serving her husband and kids. As she shared her prayer of intention with me, it was obvious that something beautiful had been rekindled in her life.

In the months that followed Madeline's meditation on the Kingdom Exercise, she shared with me her periodic returns to it. She understood that growing in her awareness of Christ's companionship with her in the ordinary moments of life was not a quick fix, but rather, a spiritual gift to cultivate throughout the rest of her life. Repeatedly returning to it in prayer has offered her further insights into how Christ is with her, how she is responding to his presence, what she loves most about him, and what he loves most about her. That deepening companionship continues to spill over into her relationship with her husband and kids in ways that have blessed and influenced them. It has helped Madeline to realize that she has a deep desire for her life to be a lived poem of love that pleases Christ and her family.

If the difficult circumstances you're experiencing right now have left you feeling lonely, exhausted, and disconnected, then taking time to prayerfully renew your awareness of Christ's companionship, as well as your awareness of the companionship of others, can rekindle your passion and wholeheartedness. It won't be easy, though. The path of least resistance is almost always a path of self-absorption and self-reliance. In fact, our culture constantly promotes a form of isolationism that disdains the notion of connecting with God and others. To break out of that cultural self-focus requires hard spiritual work and deep humility. Rather than going it alone until the darkness of loneliness and disconnection overtakes us, Ignatius encourages us to take the path less traveled by remembering who is with us and cultivating the vulnerable intimacy of that companionship.

PATHS TO COMPANIONSHIP WITH CHRIST

As I mentioned in the introduction, there are too many books that talk about wholeheartedness without offering practical and tangible paths to experiencing it. Therefore, I offer paths to wholeheartedness at the end of each chapter. I consider these parts of the book to be the most important because they move beyond other people's stories and connect the *Spiritual Exercises* to *your* story. I hope that you will take time in personal prayer to use the suggestions at the end of each chapter to rekindle authentic passion and wholeheartedness in every area of your life, especially the circumstances that are the most difficult.

Let's begin with applying the three parts of the Kingdom Exercise to your life. I recommend that you consider spending twenty to sixty minutes in prayer for each of the three parts. You can also spread the meditation out over a longer period of time—days or weeks. Regardless of how much time you devote to this meditation, begin by finding a quiet and comfortable place for prayer. Ask the Holy Spirit to guide your prayer. Then, closing your eyes and using your imagination, think of a person whom you deeply admire. Imagine being invited by him or her to do something that fills your heart with excitement and joy! Take as much time as you can to imagine *every* detail—what you see, hear, smell, touch, and taste. Give yourself plenty of time to *feel*; you might even want to write down in your prayer journal the most meaningful feelings you experience during this part of the meditation.

When you sense that you have finished imagining that fictional scenario, move to the second part of the Kingdom Exercise by replacing the person you admire with Christ. Let the scenario itself remain the same. In other words, if the first part of your meditation involved being invited to a poetry conference, then let Christ invite you to the same thing in this second part of the meditation. Once again, imagine every single detail as vividly as possible and stay aware of the emotions—the affective movements—that you feel, even making note of them in your journal. One good indication that you're coming to the end of this second part of the meditation is when you feel a powerful response to Christ's invitation welling up within you. By the end of this part, it will no longer make sense to respond to Christ's invitation and love with, "Uh-huh," but rather, "I love you!"

Having taken the second part of the Kingdom Exercise as deep as you feel like you can, move to the third and last part—the prayer of intention. In your prayer journal, write a specific response and commitment to Christ that has surfaced from your companionship with him in this meditation. You might spend several prayer times writing and editing your response so that it is as vulnerable, honest, and courageous as possible. Then, apply that prayer of intention to the specific area of your life where you've been feeling half-hearted, lonely, and disconnected. Let the passion of being in companionship with Christ take tangible form in your desolate circumstance.

Going through the Kingdom Exercise in this way may take many prayer times and will more than likely be something that you go back to numerous times during your life when you need to rekindle wholeheartedness in various circumstances. After completing the Kingdom Exercise on any given occasion, however, if you find yourself still desiring to cultivate the wholeheartedness and passion of companionship, then I recommend using Ignatius' colloquy prayer. He explains the colloquy at the beginning of the *Exercises*, writing, "The colloquy is made by speaking exactly as one friend speaks to another" (#54). In other words, the colloquy reverences that we're not alone by inviting us to talk with various saints or members of the Trinity just as we would a friend. While that might seem a bit daunting, you'll discover, as Dana did, that it's really quite simple.

Dana has been one of my directees for eleven years. She recently shared with me that she was feeling "frustrated, exhausted, and disconnected" serving as her mom's primary caregiver. Her mother had fallen and broken her hip and none of Dana's siblings were making any effort to help. The full weight of the caregiving fell to Dana and she was feeling increasingly alone and disconnected. At the very moment she reached the end of her rope, God inspired her with a profound awareness of companionship that changed everything.

In a particularly dark moment of exhaustion and loneliness, Dana found herself doing a colloquy with Jesus, sharing with him her desolation more vulnerably and deeply than ever before. In the quiet moment that followed her sharing and tears, Christ reminded Dana of the story in the Gospel of Matthew, chapter twenty-five, where he says, "Amen, I say to you, whatever you did for one of these least brothers of mine, you did for me" (25:40). While that might seem like a simple or even pietistic reminder to you and me, Dana felt something meaningful stir in her heart as she remembered those words.

Dana realized that she was not alone. Christ was in her and in her mom. She was literally being given an opportunity to serve Christ as Christ. As she spent several days meditating on that Scripture story and continuing her colloquy with Christ, she explained to me that she was experiencing a renewed willingness, generosity, and availability. Most surprisingly, though, she experienced a renewed joy in serving her mom.

While it wasn't specifically the Kingdom Exercise that helped Dana, it was certainly the companionship that the Kingdom Exercise calls us to experience. Through the colloquy that Ignatius recommends, Dana was able to connect with Christ in vulnerable intimacy and rekindle her passion for serving her mother. That is the power of companionship. Like Dana, you might find it very meaningful to vulnerably and deeply share with Christ, as with a close friend, what you are experiencing in the difficult circumstance that is draining passion and meaning from your life. If so, remember to give Christ a chance to respond to your sharing, whether through a Scripture story or through the Holy Spirit whispering in your heart; that's what makes it a colloquy rather than a soliloquy.

As you use the Kingdom Exercise and the colloquy to meditate on companionship with God, please remember that your focus must shift from the details and loneliness of your painful circumstances to how you and Christ are with one another. For most of us, that shift will be very difficult because we are used to minimizing prayer to simply telling Jesus how we need him to fix various circumstances. It might be completely new for you to let prayer be a savoring of how Christ is with you and how you are with him. The more you and I do that, however, the more we realize that the circumstances of life are always secondary to the gift and power of companionship.

CHAPTER TWO

Wholeheartedness in the Beginning

The Infancy Narratives

I spent the summer of 1998 in Cuernavaca, Mexico trying to learn Spanish. While it didn't go well, it provided me with a lifetime of stories. Some of those memories are traumatic, like lying in a pool of my own vomit begging God to take my life because I had foolishly eaten a homemade popsicle from a street vendor. Some of the stories are funny, like thinking my host family had named their dog "Dookie" because I hadn't yet learned the Spanish word "*Duque*" (which means "Duke," rather than poop). Surprisingly, some of the stories are both traumatic and funny, like my misadventure to the cathedral.

I really stepped out of my comfort zone when I chose to take a public transit bus across town to the cathedral all by myself, especially considering I didn't own a cell phone or a

GPS. As an introvert, the idea of navigating through the city's half a million people was scary, but I tried to stay positive. "What's the worst thing that could happen?" I asked myself. After all, the buses took circular routes through town, so the worst scenario I could imagine was simply ending up back where I started and not finding the cathedral. Filled with hope, I hopped on the bus, which looked like an old bread truck, except it had narrow bench seats and small windows. Since none of the seats provided adequate legroom, I sat in the very back of the bus with my long legs spilling out into the aisle.

As the bus approached downtown, I diligently looked for the bell towers of the cathedral. Unfortunately, tall buildings and lots of hills obscured my view. I didn't see the church, and the bus continued on its way, leaving downtown. Assuming we were heading back to where we came from, I felt discouraged that I didn't get to visit the church. My discouragement turned to concern, however, when the bus left Cuernavaca. Since I wasn't conversant in Spanish (and I was also a stereotypical man who rarely asked for directions or help), I sat on the hot bus convincing myself that we were going to pick up passengers just outside of the city and then head back to where I had boarded. Instead, we came to another town. My concern grew with each passing stop as the bus left that town and headed to two others.

Now, more than two hours away from Cuernavaca, armed with only enough Spanish to order a beer and ask for the location of a bathroom, I began to panic. In fact, I was so unsettled about being lost that I failed to notice that I was the only passenger left on the bus. That realization came quickly, however, when the bus turned into what I assume was the bus driver's driveway and came to a stop. As the driver exited the bus, he suddenly saw me. While I don't know what he was saying, he seemed extremely angry that I had followed him home. In a sheepish voice, I kept saying over and over, "Cuernavaca," and "cathedral," putting my hands together in the shape of a church steeple. The bus driver also used hand gestures, which I interpreted to mean, "Get off my bus!"

I felt unsettled and lost. I knew that arrogantly forging forward as if I intended to leave Cuernavaca was no longer an option. I needed to get back to the beginning—to where I started. I am not just talking about returning to the bus stop where my misadventure began. I recognized that it was even more important for me to get back to the hope-filled and wholehearted disposition I felt at the beginning of the journey. While this might sound a bit crazy, my desire to get back to how I was *feeling* at the beginning of my misadventure was even more important to me than fixing my unfortunate circumstance. I didn't want to feel frazzled and unsettled; I desired peace again.

Leaving the bus, I wandered through an unfamiliar and busy neighborhood until I came to a bus stop. Amazingly, the next bus that arrived was heading to Cuernavaca. Boarding the bus, I sat in an uncomfortable seat near the front. Despite the pain of being wedged in a seat that seemed built for a child, I felt a deep relief knowing that I was headed back to where I started, to a place that was familiar and full of hope and potential. That's how it often is when we find ourselves off course—peace and hope reveal themselves as we move back to the beginning.

If you're feeling unsettled and lost right now due to circumstances in your life, then you might know what I mean; trying to change our circumstances often has to be secondary to changing our interior disposition and focus. The game of golf is a great analogy. I played golf on my day off each week for many years. I was a double-bogey golfer, which, for those of you not familiar with the game, means I was not very good. Many of my shots missed their intended target. However, rather than finding my golf ball and physically taking it back to the place I hit the last shot, I would try to get back to the emotional and mental place of peace I enjoyed before that horrible shot, hoping that my renewed disposition would help to get the next shot back into the fairway. Without returning to the emotional and mental state of peace and focus, I would become increasingly frustrated and my score would end up looking more like my blood pressure reading.

My experience in Cuernavaca, as well as the game of golf, helped teach me that, at the moments in our lives when we're feeling the most unsettled and lost, it's important to return to the beginning rather than forging forward. Returning to a particular starting place, whether it is a physical, mental, emotional, or spiritual place, can provide profound clarity, purpose, and wholeheartedness. This is true in all circumstances in our lives, not just traumatic misadventures or inconsequential hobbies. For example, I discovered a renewed sense of purpose and passion for a youth ministry presentation by returning to the beginning.

The youth minister at a parish an hour from my house contacted me and asked if I would offer a presentation on the seven gifts of the Holy Spirit. I eagerly accepted her invitation and looked forward to the opportunity. For several weeks, I worked on the presentation, building a PowerPoint slide show, looking for accompanying music, researching icebreakers, and creating a workbook for the kids. The more I prepared for the class, however, the more I felt spiritually unsettled, lost, and anxious. I felt my initial excitement about the ministry opportunity slowly draining out of me.

My personal prayer time became consumed with worrying about the presentation and asking God for help. It was during prayer that I sensed God inviting me back to the beginning. A question surfaced in my spirit, "Were you invited to share about the gifts of the Holy Spirit or put together a PowerPoint presentation, accompanying music, icebreakers, activities, and a workbook?" I realized that I had put more pressure and work on myself than necessary; I had gone off course in preparing for the youth ministry class. That simple question during prayer helped me to spiritually go back to the moment the youth director asked me to do the presentation.

As I reflected on her invitation, I realized that my enthusiasm wasn't rooted in putting together great materials and activities; it was simply sharing my passion for God. As I spiritually and emotionally returned to the beginning of that ministry opportunity, I felt a rekindling of my passion, which bore good fruit when I eventually taught the class. The presentation went very well; I was vulnerable with the teens, speaking from my heart rather than hiding behind the distracting trappings of technology and clever activities. The students responded well and seemed sincerely engaged during the class. What would the class have been like had I pushed forward and focused more on the *medium* of the content rather than on the *content* itself?

When you and I feel unsettled and lost in life, then it's time to return to the beginning. As you can imagine, it takes great humility to spiritually, emotionally, and sometimes even physically turn around and go back to the beginning of a particular circumstance in order to experience a renewed awareness of the direction that will allow us to be our most authentic and wholehearted self. Yet, there is no other healthy response to those moments in life when we are heading down the wrong path. Not only have my own experiences confirmed that truth, so have the *Spiritual Exercises*. In them, Ignatius offers us an amazing spiritual tool that can help us to return to and reminisce about the beginning of a particular part of our life story in a way that deepens the wholeheartedness we desire. One of my directees, Eugene, learned firsthand the transforming power of returning to the beginning through Ignatius' meditation.

Eugene and I have known each other for about eight years, and he's been coming to spiritual direction every month for most of that time. About two years ago, I noticed some changes in him. He no longer prayed regularly and he seemed emotionally disconnected during our sessions. As months unfolded, he seemed more and more depressed. One day, during our time together, Eugene addressed his lethargy, asking, "Is God calling me to a new job?" He went on to explain that he was unhappy working for the police department and wondered if God was asking him to change careers.

Eugene was unsettled and lost. Many of us know that feeling. Maybe you're experiencing something very similar right now in your life. Has a difficult circumstance led you to consider making a significant change? Before you read about Eugene's struggles, I encourage you to pause for a moment and be aware of your own feelings. What does that darkness, or what Ignatius calls desolation, feel like in your life right now? What is it that you want to change about your life?

Since Ignatius recommends that we never make a major change while we're experiencing desolation, I encouraged Eugene to avoid a quick decision. Instead, I invited him to spend time in prayer with a section of the *Exercises* that focuses on the childhood of Christ. Eugene responded skeptically to my recommendation, obviously wondering what Jesus' childhood had to do with his depression and his desire for change. I explained that meditating on Jesus' earthly beginning was a wonderful opportunity for him to remember the beginning of his police career. Despite his skepticism, Eugene agreed to meditate on Jesus' incarnation, birth, and early childhood, but he wanted some suggestions on how to start. Thankfully, Ignatius offers some great suggestions, including two methods for imaginatively meditating on Scripture.

Imaginative prayer was clearly Ignatius' favorite style of meditation, but just the name alone—imaginative prayer—stirs up fear in many of us. I've heard people express their aversion to imaginative prayer (even before they learned what it entails), saying, "I don't have a good imagination." Thankfully, this style of prayer doesn't require an amazing imagination or extraordinary creativity. It only requires our availability; the rest is God's work. I firmly believe that when God desires for us to use imaginative prayer, God will give us the grace to experience it. Also, I believe that this style of prayer is easier when we think of it as simply *reminiscing* about something that has already happened, rather than feeling like we have to *imagine something completely new*. I've found that most people are much more receptive to and relaxed about reminiscing compared to imagining. That is what I explained to Eugene before I taught him the two methods of imaginative prayer.

The first method of imaginative prayer that Ignatius describes in the *Exercises* entails visualizing that we are in heaven with the Trinity looking down upon the events taking place on earth. As we do, we not only pay attention to what we're witnessing, but also how we feel. Additionally, we remain aware of how each member of the Trinity reacts to the events. The most challenging part of the meditation is not the imagining, but rather seeing things from God's perspective, especially since we live in a culture that often abhors viewing events and experiences from anyone's perspective other than one's own. It takes a great deal of humility and courage to wade through the distorting muck of our own egos and choose to see the events of life from another's perspective. This is precisely what Peter was struggling with when Jesus said to him, "Get behind me, Satan! You are an obstacle to me. You are thinking not as God does, but as human beings do" (Matthew 16:23).

Even though this first method of imaginative prayer can be challenging, it's very important for us to ask God for the grace to experience it, and then spend time using it during personal prayer. If you're wondering where to start, Ignatius encourages us to begin with the Incarnation. We are invited to place ourselves with the Father and the Holy Spirit, looking down upon the earth at the moment the Word became flesh. As we do, we allow ourselves to share God's perspective on that crucial moment in salvation history, and we enter into the hope and joy of the moment. We might think of this as being similar to the intimacy family members experience as they celebrate an important event together. During the prayer, we experience intimacy with God through our shared experience of the Second Person of the Trinity entering our earthly condition.

The second method of imaginative prayer is used much more frequently in the *Exercises*. It involves prayerfully placing ourselves in the various stories of Jesus' life. We begin this method by reading a particular Bible story a few times, familiarizing ourselves with the details. Then, we set the Bible aside, close our eyes, and let the Holy Spirit direct our imaginations, similar to how a movie director would handle characters and scenes. With the Spirit directing the story, we let it freely unfold in our imaginations. Once again, we might find it easier to approach this style of prayer as if we are reminiscing about something that we have already experienced rather than trying to imagine something completely new.

An important part of this method of imaginative prayer is to willingly and gently let the Holy Spirit cast us as a character in the story. Maybe we are a main character or simply a bystander. Regardless of our role, we ask God for the grace to let the story unfold in the way the Spirit desires, even if it is different from the account in the gospels. While we might feel a bit suspect and skeptical about using our imaginations in this way, Ignatius believed that God speaks to our hearts through the features, details, and feelings we experience in this style of prayer. As the Holy Spirit directs the scene, we are invited to trustingly pay attention to what we see, smell, hear, touch, taste, and say, believing that God will reveal meaningful insights to us through those details.

This style of prayer requires us to deeply trust God and let go of our expectations and analytical thinking. For example, one of the first times I practiced imaginative prayer, I found myself standing in front of the manger that held the newborn Christ. As I looked around, I noticed that everyone was focused on Jesus except for Joseph, who was talking on a cell phone. Rather than slip into analytical thinking, which would have caused me to scoff at the idea of a cell phone being part of a first-century story, I let the Holy Spirit continue to direct the prayer time. To make a long story short, God used Joseph's cell phone to teach me about how often I get wrapped up in side-conversations that take my focus off of Christ. That's the blessing of imaginative prayer, it doesn't have to make historical, technological, or scientific sense; we simply trust God and stay in our hearts, receiving what we are being shown and taught.

Not only can we use both of these methods of meditation to reflect on Christ's story, we can also use them to reflect on the beginning of our vocation or the important decisions we desire to rekindle. As we do, God has an opportunity to show us what our passion, willingness, and magnanimity looked like in the beginning when we first chose a particular vocation or made an important choice. That insight will give us greater clarity about how to grow in wholeheartedness, which is precisely what Eugene discovered when he humbly agreed to meditate on the infancy narratives in the gospels.

Eugene struggled at first with imaginative prayer. In fact, as he meditated on the first few stories of Jesus' life, his prayer felt dry and empty. Eugene's experience during prayer changed, however, when he got to the story about the magi visiting the baby Jesus. Using the first style of imaginative prayer, Eugene pictured himself sitting in heaven with the Father and the Holy Spirit as they watched the story of the magi unfold. He felt an intense consolation during the experience, which seemed to come from his awareness of how intently the Father, the Holy Spirit, and the magi focus on Jesus. The prayer moved Eugene's heart in a surprising way, and he suddenly realized that what he felt was a passion similar to the one he experienced at work in the months following his graduation from the police academy.

Viewing the Bible story from God's perspective, Eugene noticed for the first time in his life that the magi were focused on finding a *person*, rather than an object or a task. He suddenly realized that the main reason he became a police officer was to connect with people in his community. The primary thing he loved about being a police officer was the opportunity to meet new people every day. That changed three years ago when he took a promotion that put him behind a desk in a small cubicle. During prayer, reflecting on Jesus' beginning and his own beginning with the police department, Eugene understood that it was the move from patrolling the streets to pushing papers that marked an almost imperceptible path to unsettledness, half-heartedness, and depression.

Eugene's prayer helped him discern that he did not want to quit police work, but rather, he desired to get back to the streets. He desired to return to the one thing that, from the beginning, made him passionate about being a police officer—connecting with the people he served and protected. Thankfully, in the months following his revelation in prayer, Eugene was offered an opportunity to change positions in his department and get back on patrol. He felt happier, more connected to God and others, and more passionate. He experienced an increased generosity and availability at work for the first time in several years. Eugene felt like himself again, and that's an amazing gift. Let's be honest, it's a gift that many of us desire.

The challenges and chaos of life can often throw us off course, pulling us away from our most authentic self and draining meaning and passion from our lives. Like Eugene, we long to feel like ourselves again, to feel alive. In order to connect to that wholeheartedness, we sometimes have to return to the beginning, to the wellspring of our life's passion. Five hundred years before Eugene discovered that truth, Ignatius experienced it by spiritually and emotionally returning to the beginning of his intimate relationship with God. The interior place he returned to wasn't the conversion he experienced at Loyola, but it was five particularly meaningful spiritual experiences he had during prayer at Manresa. But I'm getting ahead of myself.

After his leg injury and subsequent conversion, Ignatius left Loyola in 1522 AD and traveled more than three hundred miles to Montserrat, arriving on the feast of Saint Benedict. He decided to travel across Europe and then on to Jerusalem so that he could connect more intimately with Christ by spending time at holy shrines. He detoured to the monastery at Montserrat, however, to formally renounce his past sins and commit his journey and life to the Blessed Virgin Mary.

Upon leaving the vestiges of his secular life as a soldier at the altar in Montserrat, he continued his trek toward Barcelona where he hoped to board a ship eastward toward the Holy Land. Unexpectedly, Ignatius was further delayed from his destination when he stopped in Manresa, which is between Montserrat and Barcelona. That stop turned into a very important yearlong pause in his journey; it became the "beginning"—the wellspring—that Ignatius spiritually and emotionally returned to throughout his life to rekindle his life's passion and grow in wholeheartedness.

While sleeping at the small Santa Lucia hospital each night, Ignatius spent his days begging for his meals in town and praying in a cave outside of town that overlooked the valley of the Cardoner River. Those days were meaningful and pivotal because of numerous spiritual experiences, which Ignatius describes in his autobiography. While all the experiences were different, they all revealed the same important message—that God deeply loved Ignatius and desired to grow in mutual love with him. Those epiphanies were so profound and life-changing that Ignatius compared every other experience to them for the rest of his life. In his autobiography, he writes that the consolations and blessings he received from God were "like those which he had been [accustomed] to receive at Manresa." Ignatius' autobiography, as well as the *Spiritual Exercises*, makes it clear that the spiritual experiences at Manresa were a "beginning" that he reminisced about often, savoring their message and wholeheartedly responding to their invitation into intimacy with God.

What is the "beginning" that you reminisce about when you're struggling? Maybe you've never asked or answered that question, but doing so is a wonderful avenue toward wholehearted living.

I encourage you to be as vulnerable and courageous as Eugene and Ignatius as you take time over the next few days to reflect on three things—Jesus' beginning, the beginning of the vocation or decision you desire to rekindle, and your response to what God reveals to you. In fact, you might want to spend one prayer time on each of those three parts, returning to that beautiful beginning and source of grace that can rekindle your life's passion and lead to wholehearted living.

PATHS TO THE BEGINNING

If spiritually and emotionally returning to the beginning of the difficult circumstance in your life feels overwhelming, don't worry. Here are some practical suggestions for your personal prayer time before we move to the next chapter. The first thing I recommend is taking time to reflect on the beginning of Jesus' life. Not only does Ignatius recommend this meditation, but I've also found that there are important aspects of Jesus' beginning that can teach us about our own beginning. Some of the Scripture stories that Ignatius recommends that we reflect on include Jesus' incarnation (Luke 1:26–38), his birth (Matthew 1:18–25; Luke 2:1–14), the shepherds' visit (Luke 2:15–20), the magi's visit (Matthew 2:1–12), the presentation in the temple (Luke 2:22–38), Mary and Joseph finding Jesus in the temple (Luke 2:41–52), and the flight to Egypt (Matthew 2:13–23).

As you take time in prayer using either or both styles of imaginative prayer, ask the Holy Spirit to show you the commonalities between Jesus' beginning and the beginning of the circumstance in your life that has become difficult. As you notice those similarities, allow God to help you return to the beginning—to the wellspring of grace—and be renewed in generosity, passion, willingness, availability, and wholeheartedness. For example, one of my directees, Scott, found renewal in his marriage as he reflected on Mary and Joseph finding Jesus in the temple. During prayer, Scott was struck by a specific detail—that Mary and Joseph did not sit back and wait for their vocation to haphazardly unfold, but they were *proactive* in parenting, actively seeking to find the child, Jesus. He realized that, after six years of marriage, he was living in a *reactive* way rather than proactively loving his wife. Based on that revelation, Scott chose to be more like he was in the beginning of his marriage—looking for practical ways to preemptively love his wife. Like Scott, as you apply some of the dynamics of Jesus' story to your own, let it draw you back to the wholeheartedness you experienced in the beginning.

Next, I recommend that you enjoy some personal prayer times imaginatively being with the Trinity in heaven as they look down upon the younger version of yourself at the moment you made the important decision or entered into the vocation with which you're currently struggling. During that meditation, be aware of how you and each member of the Trinity feel about that moment in your life. As you reminisce about the beginning, where do you see wholeheartedness and passionate generosity? When did you begin feeling unsettled and lost, and what caused those feelings? Those are some very difficult questions to reflect on, so please be patient with yourself and know that you might need to return to that meditation multiple times over the course of many days or weeks.

Lastly, it is important that we take time to reflect on our response to what God shows us in prayer. It would not have been enough for Eugene to learn that he needed to get back to the community he loved to serve. He also had to respond to that realization by looking for an opportunity to get back on patrol. Similarly, it was not enough for Scott to realize that his love for his wife needed to be proactive again; it was essential for him to find practical, tangible ways to put that information into action. The same is true for us. Until we respond to what God has shown us in prayer, it is merely information, rather than transformation. And let's be honest, no one has ever become wholehearted through information in the head without transformation in the heart. I recommend that you spend a few prayer times sharing with God how you would like to respond to what you learned while meditating on the beginning of Christ's life and the beginning of your decision.

As you spend time prayerfully returning to the beginning of the vocation or decision in which you desire greater passion and wholeheartedness, trust that God was with you in the beginning and God is with you now. Regardless of how far off the path we feel like we've wandered, God is with us. Look at how far King David strayed from who he was as a boy, and yet he remained God's chosen one and God remained close to him. While David could not magically rewind his circumstances and change many of the things that happened, he was able to spiritually and emotionally return to the wholeheartedness he experienced as a boy. The same is true for us. No matter how unsettled and lost we become in life, there is always an opportunity to spiritually and emotionally return to the beginning and find renewal.

CHAPTER THREE

Wholeheartedness through Compassion

The Two Standards

Suffering not only has the power to destroy our passion and joy, but it can also isolate us. Deep hurt often brings about deep loneliness. I learned that when I left the priesthood; nothing could have prepared me for the profound alienation I experienced. I naively thought that my discernment would be received with understanding since it was based on a sincere and long journey through the *Spiritual Exercises.* Don't get me wrong—I expected that many of my brother priests would be disappointed, just as I had been in the past when I heard of men leaving the priesthood. However, I expected that they would reach out to me as I had done for the priests who took leaves of absence before me. The bishop seemed to share my hope, telling me to expect several of my brother priests to reach out to me once the news of my leave of absence was announced. Instead of calls and emails, though, there was silence.

Maybe my brother priests were so deeply hurt by my decision that they distanced themselves. Or, maybe they were so overworked and burned out that they didn't have the energy to reach out. Regardless of the reasons, all of the hurtful silence was incarnated in one particular priest—a man who had served as one of my mentors. I ran into him at several diocesan events following the announcement of my leave of absence and he physically turned his back on me, refusing to acknowledge or talk to me. That brought about a darkness so suffocating that it squelched my hope, energy, and passion, and left me feeling abandoned.

My path out of that darkness toward the wholeheartedness that I desired began with family members, friends, and former parishioners reaching out to me with support, love, and prayers. Their kindness and gentleness after hearing about my leave of absence brought some light to the darkness and helped confirm the truth I shared in chapter one—that companionship can help rekindle our life's passion. However, my desolation was so deep that I needed more than loving companionship. Thankfully, God helped me to see that I was being invited into a *deeper* companionship called compassion.

Compassion is different than the empathy of ordinary companionship. The latter involves simply being aware of how the other person is *feeling,* while the former is a deep sharing in a similar *condition of suffering.* The word compassion literally means *to suffer with* and, therefore, the most meaningful forms of compassion involve people who share very similar painful circumstances and struggles. Such compassion is extremely important because, when we're willing to acknowledge the pain of our circumstances and let it connect us to others who are in similar painful situations, it can pull us out of the isolation of suffering and lead us toward wholeheartedness. That is what I experienced when I made the decision to reach out to other men who had left the priesthood.

When I wasn't busy offering spiritual direction or writing, I took time to call, email, and message men from our diocese who left the priesthood during the years that I served in Arkansas. I listened to their stories and shared mine. Rather than isolating myself, I let my pain compassionately draw me to others who were hurting in similar ways. I found that even the men who left ordained ministry many years ago still had residual hurt and resentment. They needed opportunities to share their feelings and connect with someone who understood. I needed that same gift.

Compassionately connecting with those men inspired me to do the same with Christ. I began spending some of my personal prayer time vulnerably sharing with Christ how I was feeling and letting my hurt connect me with stories in his life where people alienated him. As I meditated on gospel stories like Peter denying his friendship with Jesus, I continued the movement out of the isolation of suffering and into a more meaningful connectedness, which led to healing and helped me rediscover passion. During those prayer times, I sensed that Christ was grateful for my compassion, just as I was grateful for his.

When have you recently felt desolate, alone, or victimized? Does the circumstance that you brought to God at the beginning of this book leave you feeling that way? It's impossible to live wholeheartedly and passionately when we're feeling desolate and alone. Thankfully, Ignatius offers us a pathway out of the darkness through the gift of compassion, which is illustrated in a meditation known as the Two Standards, found in Week Two of the *Spiritual Exercises*. The meditation reminds us that bonds of compassion are extremely strong; they can draw us out of the loneliness of suffering and into a meaningful communion with Christ and others.

The Two Standards meditation is primarily meant to teach us to model our lives on the life of Christ for the sake of evangelization. However, my second time through the *Exercises* helped me to see that this meditation also invites us to experience compassion with Christ that leads to wholeheartedness. If you're not acquainted with this meditation, Ignatius draws once again from the experiences with which he was familiar—the military. He invites us to prayerfully imagine two opposing armies preparing for battle. The one army is led by Satan and follows his military banner or standard, while Jesus Christ is the general in charge of the second army led by his standard. We are asked to imaginatively experience every detail of the staging of that epic battle. Basically, we're being invited by Ignatius to imaginatively enter into the Armageddon described in chapter sixteen of the Book of Revelation.

As we prayerfully enter that battle scene on the biblical plain of Megiddo, it might seem logical to assume that the purpose of the meditation is to remember to choose good over evil, to follow Jesus rather than Satan, but Ignatius had a different and deeper purpose in mind. The meditation first prompts us to recall that Christ has chosen us as his servants and friends. As we learned in the Kingdom Exercise, being chosen by Jesus and being with him is, in and of itself, an opportunity to grow in passion and wholeheartedness. Then, this new meditation challenges us to experience and feel the same things that Jesus experienced and felt during his earthly ministry, including humiliation, poverty, and the world's contempt. In other words, we are invited to *suffer with* Christ.

Ignatius points out that one of the reasons why we would choose to suffer with Christ is to evangelize. Being compassionately connected with Christ in his suffering is an effective way to share the gospel because we aren't merely preaching with words; we're *living* the unique image of Christ that we were created to be for the world. As such, we are incarnations of the gospel. Additionally, suffering with Christ (and letting him suffer with us) is a deep form of intimacy. By allowing our experience of poverty, humiliation, and the world's contempt to touch Christ's poverty, humiliation, and the world's contempt, we are no longer alone and the storehouse of intimacy, passion, and wholeheartedness is opened for us. That is the power of compassion. As you might imagine, that power is in no way limited to the three things that Ignatius mentions in the meditation—poverty, humility, and the world's contempt. It can include any form of compassion, which I realized a couple of years ago as I listened to the story of Diego and José.

The very first time I saw the video of ten-year-old Diego Mercado doing CrossFit with José Luis Sanchez, a marine who lost his leg in Afghanistan, I was overwhelmed with empathy. When the video ended, I looked up their story online and learned that they met when Diego attended a Ride 2 Recovery wounded warrior event. Diego's dad explained that, "As [the wounded warriors] passed, they saw Diego with a prosthetic [leg] sitting out front, and one by one, they stopped." José was one of the soldiers who stopped to greet Diego. He felt compassion for the boy who, despite having only one leg, hopes to be a soldier when he grows up. It was evident in the video that the two of them forged a compassionate bond through their shared condition of suffering. Their friendship fueled their passion for helping others, leading Diego to establish his own non-profit to help others with disabilities. Rather than letting his suffering isolate him, compassionately connecting with José led him to greater passion and wholeheartedness. The same thing happened to my friend Steven.

Steven struggled with alcoholism for many years before getting sober in Alcoholics Anonymous. After years of sobriety, he recently agreed to serve as a sponsor, companioning with others on their path to sobriety. While those of us who have never struggled with alcoholism can *empathize* with what that addiction might feel like, Steven feels a deep *compassion* for those whom he sponsors. He personally knows the hopelessness, shame, and self-hatred that are part of the disease. He courageously chose to let his painful experiences compassionately connect him with others in a way that has allowed him to be, in his own words, "a better man because of it." I purposely describe Steven's compassion as courageous because it is very difficult for most of us to allow our own painful experiences to connect us with others who are in a similar struggle. Such courageous compassion is not nearly as commonplace as isolation, which is how many of us choose to handle our pain.

As I mentioned earlier, our natural response to suffering is to recoil, withdrawing inward where we can become despondent, angry, isolated, and even inconsiderate of others. It takes a tremendous amount of love and courage to choose to let our suffering lead us outward into compassion. Diego and José clearly have that courage, and it's demonstrated in the work they do with children and veterans with disabilities. Steven also has that courage, and it's manifested in his ministry in Alcoholics Anonymous. How are you courageously using your suffering and desolation to compassionately connect you with Christ and others?

Rather than feeling victimized and powerless in the painful and uncontrollable circumstances of life, Ignatius teaches us how to grow in wholeheartedness through compassion with Christ. Regardless of what type of suffering we're experiencing, Christ has already experienced something similar, which means we can offer to him, as well as receive from him, the gift of compassion in that painful circumstance. Let me repeat that—it doesn't matter what form our suffering takes, Christ has already experienced something similar, which means that we can offer to him, as well as receive from him, the gift of compassion in that painful circumstance. Take a moment to let that profound truth sink in.

What leaves you feeling victimized and powerless? Maybe it involves sickness, grief, joblessness, divorce, a child who often gets in trouble, a spouse who isn't your best friend, or a painful loss. Pause for a moment and share your thoughts and feelings about it with God. Ignatius understood that when life leaves us feeling victimized and powerless, we often can't change the circumstances, but we can prayerfully discover the similarities that our situation has in common with Christ's experiences. That compassion and connectedness can rekindle the passion and wholeheartedness that we desire.

One of the circumstances in Ignatius' life that left him feeling victimized and powerless was his arrest. After finally making it to the Holy Land, Ignatius' stay was cut short because of the persecution and threats Christians faced in Jerusalem at that time. Disappointed, Ignatius headed back to Barcelona in 1524 AD to study at the university. Having arrived in Venice, he walked toward Genoa where he met some Spanish soldiers. They explained that the route Ignatius was traveling was dangerous because it would lead him near the French army. They encouraged him to take a safer route, but Ignatius ignored their advice.

In his autobiography, Ignatius describes how his route took him directly into the presence of French soldiers who thought he was a spy and arrested him. Despite repeated explanations that he was simply journeying to Barcelona to study, they stripped him of his clothing and searched his shoes and cloak for hidden codes. Then they led him half-naked through the main streets of the village to the army captain.

Ignatius' situation was clearly out of his control, and his hope for a safe journey to Barcelona was crushed. He was paraded through the city in the bitter cold of January for the amusement of the soldiers. In that experience of being victimized and powerless, Ignatius chose not to be overcome with desolation, anger, or despair, but rather, he focused his attention and prayer on the fact that he was sharing Christ's condition. He recognized his suffering as an opportunity to share compassion with Christ. Writing in the third person, Ignatius recounts the story in his autobiography.

> As he was compelled to go about in this condition, he recalled to mind the thought of Christ led about as a captive. Although he was forced to walk through the three principal streets of the town, he did so, not with sadness, but feeling great joy and consolation.

By turning his attention from the desolation of his painful and unfixable circumstances to how he shared in Christ's condition by being arrested and paraded through town, Ignatius rekindled his passion and was filled with "joy and consolation." You and I have access to the same joy and consolation despite the pain of unmet expectations in our lives. Like Ignatius, if we focus our hearts on our shared condition with Christ and others rather than on our painful circumstances, the flame of our life's passion, wholeheartedness, and magnanimity can be rekindled. That is what Jenny experienced as ALS ravaged her body.

ALS, also known as Lou Gehrig's disease, is an atrocious illness. For many victims, it begins with seemingly benign struggles, like dropping things or occasionally stumbling. However, within months, things get much worse as victims lose muscle control. This can lead to spending the last three to ten years of their lives incapable of speaking, moving their limbs, or swallowing. Additionally, people with ALS live with painful muscle cramps and twitches. All of that describes Jenny's condition when I first met her. She was confined to a wheelchair and had very little voluntary movement. Her wheelchair was designed to hold her head in place so that she could use an eye-tracking keyboard to slowly type what she could no longer speak.

I was blessed with the opportunity to bring Communion to Jenny every Friday morning for about a year and a half until her death. Since I could seldom understand the computerized voice that spoke the words Jenny typed, I sat close to her and read the words on the computer screen. She would painstakingly type one letter at a time, using her eye movement to find the letters on the keyboard, and blink to select them. Despite the fact that our conversations were painstakingly slow, they were always meaningful. Our time together was often marked by her sarcastic sense of humor, her desire to deepen her faith, and sometimes her expressions of profound pain and anger regarding her disease.

Each week seemed to bring new losses to Jenny's ability to do the simple things that most of us take for granted. Those losses left her feeling more and more victimized and powerless. During one of my visits near the end of her life, I could tell Jenny was angry and agitated about something even before she started typing. She slowly typed one letter at a time, explaining to me that her family wanted to acquire a chair lift because they could no longer pick her up to move her back and forth to the toilet. She felt humiliated and mortified at the idea of a cold metal crane picking her up. Her family explained to Jenny that they needed the lift because they loved her and could not risk accidentally dropping her. Their explanations about the practicalities of the lift did not convince Jenny, though. She remained obstinate about not using the lift.

It became apparent to me that Jenny detested the lift, at least in part because it was a visual reminder of the powerlessness she felt. I also knew that one meaningful way she would accept the lift was the same way that Ignatius found consolation in his arrest five hundred years ago—through sharing in Christ's condition. So I gently challenged Jenny to look for a way to connect the anguish of using the lift to Christ's anguish.

Through prayer and our conversations, Jenny courageously leaned into her fear and anger, focusing mainly on Christ's passion. As she did, she realized that being hoisted into the air by the lift was the closest she would ever physically come to sharing Jesus' experience on the cross. Just as he was lifted up on the wood of the cross, she too would be lifted up. While that might seem pietistic or melodramatic to some people, it was meaningful and consoling for Jenny. The lift was no longer just about *her* suffering, it became a tangible and compassionate sharing in *Christ's* suffering, which cultivated a deeper intimacy with him and provided Jenny with some consolation.

It was beautiful watching Jenny's obstinate resistance to the lift slowly dissolve as she realized that Jesus' experience of humiliation and loneliness on the cross was similar to her experience. While her prayer and new awareness did not magically erase the waves of fear, sadness, and anger, it gave her spiritual access to an intimacy with Christ and a rekindled willingness that she could not have imagined. Without realizing it, Jenny received the grace available to all of us in the Two Standards meditation—a rekindled willingness, availability, and generosity through shared compassion with Christ.

The circumstances that are pulling you into desolation do not need to be exactly like Jenny's or Ignatius' in order to benefit from the Two Standards meditation. Any unmet expectation, uncontrollable situation, or painful condition that is robbing you of passion, willingness, and wholeheartedness can be an opportunity to reach out in compassion to Christ and others who have experienced something similar. Such compassion moves us outward in love rather than recoiling in despondency and anger. I hope that you'll take time to apply some of the suggestions in the final part of this chapter to the specific painful circumstance in your life that is keeping you from the wholeheartedness you desire.

PATHS TO COMPASSION WITH CHRIST

Becoming wholehearted through the Two Standards means diving deeper into the implicit compassion we find in the meditation. More specifically, we are invited to 1) acknowledge that Christ is our amazing leader and that we desire to be more like him, 2) get to know Christ well enough to be aware of the primary conditions and experiences that marked his life, and 3) evangelize through our willingness to respond as Christ responded in those painful circumstances that we have in common with him. In the following paragraphs, I offer some new ways to become more willing, generous, and wholehearted through the compassion that is implicit in the Two Standards.

First, it's really important that we deepen our ability to feel and acknowledge our emotions. This is very difficult and will take time to develop because many people today are emotionally ignorant. This is exhibited in the fact that, culturally, our emotional vocabulary has been minimized to just a few words—happy, sad, and angry. It's also revealed in our pervasive ineptness at grieving. We frequently see people teach their children to stuff their feelings, while undiscerningly lashing out with their own feelings in outbursts like road rage. If we are to live wholehearted lives, then it is absolutely imperative that we grow in feeling deeply, acknowledging our feelings, and spiritually allowing them to connect us to Christ. Only then are we poised to experience compassion with Christ and for Christ.

I cannot stress enough the importance of us growing in our ability to accurately name our emotions, or what I like to call our affective movements. The level of specificity with which we name our emotions is proportional to the level of compassion and connectedness we will experience with Christ and others. For example, if our uncontrollable circumstances leave us feeling betrayed but we only have the emotional astuteness to say, "I'm angry," then we are going to mistakenly try to connect with Christ in our shared anger, rather than our shared experience of betrayal. As such, prayer will more than likely feel frustrating, dry, and disconnected. If, however, we are able to acknowledge the deep betrayal we feel, then we can connect with Christ in his experience of being betrayed by Judas and Peter. Simply put, the more accurately we are able to name how we feel, the more intimately we can compassionately connect with Christ in a way that manifests wholeheartedness.

In order to help my directees more accurately name their affective movements, I provide each of them with a feeling-word list when they begin spiritual direction. Personally, I keep a copy of the list in my prayer journal and refer to it when I'm feeling something but can't quite find the word to describe it. Rather than being afraid of or suspect of our emotions, Ignatius based the majority of his spirituality on both our willingness to feel deeply and our aptitude in appropriately naming those feelings. I highly recommend that you find a feeling-word list that can help you name how your circumstances are making you feel.

Knowing how we feel in various circumstances is really important, but we need more than that to compassionately connect with Christ and deepen our wholeheartedness. We also need to know when Christ experienced similar circumstances and feelings. While the Two Standards meditation focuses specifically on our compassionately sharing in Christ's condition of poverty, humility, and the world's contempt, you and I can use an internet search engine, Bible app, or concordance to find gospel stories about additional conditions and experiences that Christ shares with us. It might be a story where Jesus experienced something very similar, or simply one where he would have *felt* something similar to what we're feeling. Either way, such stories are places of compassion for us. It's a chance to know that we are not alone in how we feel and to remember that Christ not only went through what we are experiencing, but he overcame it in an eternal way, and so can we.

As we share our feelings with Christ about the painful circumstance that is robbing us of passion and wholeheartedness, and as we let Christ share with us his similar experience and feelings through a particular gospel story, we not only find meaning and passion in the intimate connection that develops between us, but we're given an opportunity to evangelize. The Two Standards meditation makes it very clear that our compassionate sharing in Christ's condition is not merely for our own passion and wholeheartedness, but it's also a meaningful way to encourage others to live the gospel. In other words, authentic compassion causes us to reach out to more and more people, intimately connecting with them rather than isolating ourselves.

The Two Standards can be so much more than a meditation on being like Christ and evangelizing. It can be a chance for you and me to become wholehearted by allowing our painful circumstances to expand our hearts in a compassion that connects us more intimately to Christ. As you take your painful situation to God in prayer, don't get bogged down by the specifics in the Two Standards meditation. Instead, simply share with Christ the feelings and details that are part of the current circumstances that cause you to feel apathetic, half-hearted, or powerless, and let Christ share with you, through the gospels, his own experiences of those feelings. Then, in the intimacy of compassion, learn from the gospels how you can respond in a passionate and wholehearted way, just as Christ did.

CHAPTER FOUR

Wholeheartedness through *Magis*

The Three Types of Persons

We live in a culture that is obsessed with *more.* The advertising industry has successfully convinced us to fear scarcity and to react to that fear by accumulating *more*—more food, more clothing, more electronics, more security, more popularity, more everything. Our obsession with more has reached an absurdity where we build larger and larger storage units and pay profuse amounts of money each month to stockpile all of the *more* we bought. As Christians, our deepening intimacy with Christ invites us to let go of the more that the world promotes and embrace a new kind of more, which Ignatius called *magis*. Not only is *magis* essential for deep friendship with Christ and others, but it is also a source of the renewed passion and wholeheartedness that we desire.

If you're familiar with Ignatian spirituality, then you've probably seen the phrase *ad majorem Dei gloriam*, or its abbreviation, AMDG. This Latin phrase translates into "for the greater glory of God" and is used by Ignatius several times in Week Two of the *Spiritual Exercises*. It's more than a slogan; it's a spiritual invitation for us to discern all of the different good things that we could choose from in any given moment and choose the one that will bring God the most glory. Ignatius believed that as we grow in intimacy with Christ, discernment will no longer be primarily about choosing something good instead of something evil, but rather, it will be choosing *the* good instead of merely *a* good. When we choose *the* good, our choice is for the greater glory of God.

A derivative of the word *majorem* in the Jesuit motto is *magis*, which means "the more" or "the greater." Before we look at how *magis* can help us live wholehearted lives, it's important to understand our motive for choosing "the more." No one chooses to do more—to go the extra mile—without a pretty deep and meaningful motive and, let's be honest, "God's glory" is not a motive meaningful enough to cause most people to be more generous. Think about that. Bringing honor to God or to anyone else is a secondary motive at best. The primary motives behind the choices that bring God the greatest glory are instead relational. They are about intimacy and vulnerability. The things that bring God *greater* glory include offering to others—and all of creation—greater love, respect, kindness, compassion, gentleness, acceptance, and mercy. When you and I sift through all of the good options in any given situation and choose the one that entails the deepest expression of vulnerable love, it is *ad majorem Dei gloriam*. Those opportunities are available numerous times each day in the ordinary events of life. The first example that comes to mind happened yesterday in our kitchen.

My wife has three towels in the kitchen. There is a hand towel, a dish-drying towel, and a decorative towel. While we were dating, I learned that it is important to her that the distinct functions of each of these towels be respected. While I don't fully grasp the importance of those distinctions, I do understand their importance to my wife. One of the ways that I can choose to love her and bring God greater glory is by using the proper kitchen towel for the function that Carmel desires. This is really important. My choosing to do the dishes is, in and of itself, an act of love that brings God glory. However, it brings God *greater* glory when I not only do the dishes but I do them in the way makes my wife feel loved and honored. Some people might think that example is too mundane or unimportant, but I assure you that *magis* is lived most profoundly in the ordinary events of life. And that is also where you and I desire to live more wholeheartedly—in the ordinary, and often challenging, circumstances of life.

Living a passionate and wholehearted life means choosing the fullness of love in every situation and circumstance. It means choosing, not just *a* good, but *the* good in each moment of the day. That can be a particularly helpful spiritual tool to use in the circumstances of our lives that cause us to feel half-hearted, complacent, and exhausted. As you might imagine, there is a certain irony to the fact that one of the things that can move us beyond our exhaustion is choosing "the more." Yet the joy we experience when we choose to love in extraordinary ways impassions us, as does the joy we experience when we feel God's delight and gratitude for our extraordinary love. That is the gift of *magis*.

Ignatius did not use the analogy of kitchen towels to illustrate the importance of *magis*; instead, he used the image of money. In his meditation, The Three Types of Persons, also known as The Three Classes of Men, he invites us to imagine that three people have been entrusted with a large sum of money. Each of them handles the money in a different way. The first person had good intentions regarding the use of the money but didn't follow through. He was all talk, no action. The second person used the money for *a* good, but not *the* good that God desired. His life was filled with love, but not the *magis* that was possible. The third person possessed the grace of holy detachment—sometimes called holy indifference—that allowed him to see himself as the steward, not the owner, of the money. This permitted him to move beyond his own superficial wants and choose *the* good that God desired and that he himself most deeply desired. As such, that person's choices regarding the money entrusted to him were made for the *greater* glory of God.

This meditation helps us to recognize the importance of the dispositions of detachment, peace, patience, freedom, and trust that are necessary to live a life of *magis*. If our decisions are primarily motivated by superficial wants, people's demands, our favorite sins, broken social structures, selfishness, shame, or regret, then we will miss opportunities for *magis*. However, when we understand ourselves to be stewards who have been entrusted by God with each moment, circumstance, and experience, then we are more deeply disposed to choose that which is "better for the service and praise of the Divine Majesty" (*Spiritual Exercises*, 155).

This meditation had such a profound impact on me while I was going through the *Exercises* the second time that I spent several months doing two important things in prayer. First, I spent a lot of time rereading the four gospels, looking for *magis* in Christ's words and actions. I sensed that *magis* is so important that it must have been incarnated in Christ's life. Sure enough, the gospels revealed numerous examples of Christ teaching and living *magis*—challenging us to choose *the* good and putting that teaching into practice.

Two of the best places we can find Jesus' teachings on *magis* are in the Sermon on the Mount (Matthew 5—7) and the Sermon on the Plain (Luke 6). In those chapters, Jesus repeatedly juxtaposes what was considered to be ordinary love and kindness with something much deeper and more meaningful. For example, he taught, "If anyone wants to go to law with you over your tunic, hand him your cloak as well. Should anyone press you into service for one mile, go with him for two miles" (Matthew 5:40–41). Simply put, in every circumstance in life, we can either do the minimum or we can choose to do the *more*.

Not only did Jesus teach about *magis* in the gospels, but he also lived it. One particularly meaningful Scripture story that I meditated on was Jesus healing the man with the withered hand. The Gospel of Luke, chapter six, tells us that while Jesus was teaching in the synagogue on the sabbath, he saw a crippled man and invited him to stand in front of the people. Jesus then asked the crowd, "Is it lawful to do good on the sabbath rather than to do evil, to save life rather than to destroy it?" (6:9). He proceeded to heal the man's hand, which caused the scribes and Pharisees to become angry because it was unlawful to heal on the sabbath. This story makes it clear that, while it is *a* good to follow religious laws, it was *the* good for Jesus to heal the man. That is *magis.* That healing was for the greater glory of God.

In addition to studying *magis* in the gospels, I reflected on how *magis* has manifested itself in my life. I found myself wondering what "more" really meant for me during various important decisions in my life. I am embarrassed to admit what I discovered. I realized that for most of my life I mistook suffering for *magis.* In other words, when I felt challenged to live more deeply for God, I assumed that the best choice—*the* good—was the one that was the biggest sacrifice and caused me the most pain. I can even see how that mentality played a role in discerning priesthood. Such glorification of suffering was deeply rooted in my theology and has only started to be healed through my deepening intimacy with God.

I know that I'm not the only person who has mistakenly connected *magis* with suffering. We Catholics are known for our suffering, even being accused of masochism at times. In our theology and spirituality we frequently extoll the unrealistic legends of ancient martyrs; we wear our own small "martyrdoms" on our sleeves; and many of us were trained to "offer up" our suffering as a gift and prayer to God. Without realizing it, we unconsciously equated suffering with honoring God. We began to believe that the more we suffer, the more it must please and honor God. However, that is not only unhealthy and untrue, but it is also not *magis*.

The heart of *magis* is not suffering for the sake of suffering, but rather, it is vulnerable intimacy. I am purposefully not describing the heart of *magis* as "love" because that word has lost much of its meaning in our culture today. Instead, I find that the phrase "vulnerable intimacy" strikes the heart more deeply and expresses what the word "love" is meant to convey. Why is *magis* an expression of vulnerable intimacy? It's because it's an expression of God. "God is love" (1 John 4:8). God's very essence is vulnerable intimacy. As such, God is openness, willingness, transparency, and authenticity. God *is* the more; therefore, it's for God's greatest glory when you and I choose to live the vulnerable intimacy that is God's very essence.

As you might imagine, choosing what is most vulnerable and intimate in every circumstance in life sometimes brings about its own suffering. To be open and available means that others can take advantage of us and deeply hurt us. However, that suffering is not masochism; we are not choosing or glorifying suffering. Instead, we are choosing vulnerable intimacy, which happens to sometimes entail suffering. This is an important theological distinction. Our theology—our God—doesn't ask us to suffer. Instead, we are asked to be vulnerably intimate, which sometimes entails suffering.

My spiritual director explained this to me on several occasions saying that the only crosses that God asks us to embrace are the ones that confirm and deepen love, that confirm and deepen vulnerable intimacy. Those are moments of *magis*.

Unfortunately, as long as various theologies view God as the Father who demanded that his Son suffer as a sacrifice for us, we will continue to equate suffering with *magis*. Tackling a healthier Christology is for another book. What is important for us right now in our understanding of *magis* is that we need to change the questions we ask when discerning the greatest good in any particular situation. Rather than asking, "Which choice will bring me the most suffering?" we should ask, "Which choice is the most vulnerable and intimate? Which choice invites me to be the most open, authentic, generous, and available?"

Living *ad majorem Dei gloriam* means choosing the greater, most vulnerable and intimate good over numerous other goods. Jesus wholeheartedly makes such choices over and over throughout the gospels and you and I are called to do the same. Through Christ's example, and the meditations in the *Exercises*, we begin to see that living a passionate and wholehearted life requires us to live *magis* at each moment of the day, including those circumstances that leave us apathetic and exhausted. Ignatius realized the same thing once he had been released from the French soldiers and made it back to Spain to begin his life as a student.

Ignatius understood that his evangelization would have a greater impact if he was able to write and communicate more effectively, which required a more formal education. So, he began studying Latin, humbly joining small children at school. In addition to his time studying, Ignatius continued to live the life that people were accustomed to witnessing—he begged for his food, prayed, did penance, taught children, visited the sick, and offered the *Exercises* to anyone who showed interest in them. As he did those things, more and more people flocked to Ignatius for his wisdom, encouragement, and help. In fact, so many people came to him that Ignatius realized he needed more than just a formal education; he needed a community.

Joining an existing religious community was an option for Ignatius, but not one that interested him. In fact, he worried that any sort of community would impact his independence and autonomy in sharing the gospel, which were goods that Ignatius valued. However, he finally realized that forming a group of men around him would be for the greater glory of God because it would mean that even more people could encounter God and be transformed through the *Exercises*. In his book *Ignatius of Loyola: The Psychology of a Saint*, W.W. Meissner explains Ignatius' decision, writing, "It became increasingly clear to [Ignatius] that his work for souls could have only limited impact as long as he tried to carry it out single-handedly. The greater good required companions who would join him in this work." Through discernment, Ignatius realized that offering the *Exercises* to people was *a* good, but offering them to hundreds of people through forming a religious community was *the* good. That choice was not only the most vulnerably intimate one, but it helped ensure that Ignatius' ministry and the impact of the *Exercises* would continue to this very day. That is the power of *magis*. When you and I choose extraordinary love, it provides us with the passion to move through challenging situations and decisions in our lives. Ellen realized the same thing as I slowly led her through the *Exercises* a couple of years ago.

Ellen's dad, James, was diagnosed with Alzheimer's in 2012. The first four years after his diagnosis were marked with a steady decline in his memory and a steady increase in his need for help. When Ellen first came to me for spiritual direction, she was clearly burned out as a caregiver. She told me that she felt complacent in helping her dad, often just doing the minimum required by her conscience. It was a horrible feeling for her to dedicate time and energy helping her dad, only to see his condition worsen. Ellen was exhausted and felt ashamed that she wished her dad would die soon. She knew she needed renewal, but she didn't know where to start; she desired to get back to the passionate and wholehearted service she offered her dad right after his diagnosis. Back then, she felt generous, patient, kind, and thoughtful. That was a long time ago and a recent incident on a Friday afternoon helped her understand just how far she had fallen in her ability to care for her dad in the way he deserved.

Her dad fell asleep in his favorite recliner shortly after lunch. Ellen's sense of relief that he was taking a nap was overshadowed by her deep depression and irritability. She went to the wet bar in the corner of the living room and grabbed the bottle of bourbon. Withdrawing to her bedroom, she began drinking. She explained to me that most of her recollection of that afternoon was a blur until she stumbled into the living room midafternoon and found her father on the floor. He had fallen and been calling for her, but she was either passed out or asleep and didn't hear him. Seeing him wincing in pain on the thin living room carpet sobered Ellen up to the truth of her burnout as a caregiver.

Ellen came to me because she knew she desired to be wholehearted again in serving as her father's caregiver. As she and I built a relationship of trust with one another in spiritual direction, I recommended that she join a caregivers' support group. I also explained to her the meditation on the Three Types of Persons and encouraged her to use it in prayer for a few weeks, imagining that it was her infirmed father, rather than a large sum of money, that was entrusted to the three people in the meditation. By this point in our relationship, Ellen knew a little about Ignatius of Loyola and was interested in trying the meditation.

As a spiritual director, I've learned not to assume that I know what God is going to communicate to people through various Scriptures and meditations. Often, as directees share with me what God taught them, or how God helped them grow, it far exceeds what I could have ever imagined. That was the case as Ellen shared with me her experiences of spending time in prayer with the Three Types of Persons. There was a gentleness and lightness that radiated from her as she entered my office and sat in the chair across from me. Even before she said a word, I knew something had changed in her.

Ellen expressed that she had taken the prayer recommendation seriously, spending about thirty minutes each day for a few weeks imagining the three persons who were entrusted with her father. She named them Heathcliff, Catherine, and Edgar, after characters in her favorite novel, *Wuthering Heights*. As the meditation unfolded in her heart, Ellen realized that the first person, Heathcliff, talked about how much he wanted to help her father, but didn't do much at all. The second person, Catherine, did a lot for her dad, but primarily the things that *she* wanted to do rather than the things that would most benefit him. I was struck by the irony that Ellen chose Catherine from *Wuthering Heights* to play the role of the middle person, since that is a similar role she played in the novel, not knowing whether she wanted to be more like Heathcliff or Edgar.

The final person in her meditation, Edgar, desired to please God more than anything else. His decisions regarding where and how he would expend his energy for Ellen's dad were based less on his own personal needs or his hope of impressing others, and more on love. Through imaginative prayer, Ellen saw that Edgar served James in vulnerable and intimate ways, which brought God *greater* glory. She was deeply moved by Edgar's response to her dad and she noticed that Edgar seemed aware that what he did for her dad he was really doing for God, and God was deeply pleased. Edgar didn't try to do everything, but focused on what love—what vulnerable intimacy—was inviting him to do in each moment. As Ellen prayerfully and imaginatively witnessed God's delight in Edgar's *magis*, she remembered Jesus' words from the Gospel of Matthew, chapter ten, "Whoever receives you receives me, and whoever receives me receives the one who sent me" (10:40).

Ellen excitedly shared with me that something finally clicked in her when she realized that she desired to serve her dad like Edgar did, finding a balance between doing too little and doing too much. She realized that the balance was achieved by doing what love invited her to do in each moment.

It was like she tapped into a deep reservoir of generosity and passion by recognizing her desire to please God. She understood more clearly the connection between the wholeheartedness of choosing vulnerable intimacy and the joy of knowing that God delighted in her and found pleasure in how she served her dad. This new awareness was a movement from doing many things with very little love to doing the one thing that Love (i.e., vulnerable intimacy) required in each moment.

The new grace that Ellen experienced was practical and tangible, not pietistic or theoretical. For example, the meditation helped Ellen to change her style of caregiving in specific ways, such as no longer arguing with her dad about what he thought was true and letting him do as much for himself as he could before she stepped in to help. She understood that those decisions were all moments of *magis. They were moments of vulnerably letting go of control and accepting the present moment.* Throughout each day, Ellen reminded herself that God had entrusted James to her and that each moment was an opportunity to be a faithful and generous steward. Each evening, she took time to acknowledge and feel God's gratitude for her, which increased her wholeheartedness and generosity.

Whether we're feeling apathetic and exhausted like Ellen, or confused about a decision we're discerning like Ignatius, or simply wanting to use the correct kitchen towel, life is filled with opportunities to choose the more and to be impassioned through those choices. Is there any particular circumstance in your life where you feel like you're doing a lot of good things, yet you feel half-hearted, complacent, or exhausted? If so, growing in *magis* can help by connecting you to the passionate joy of choosing vulnerable intimacy and the passionate pride in knowing God delights in you. In the upcoming pages, I offer some paths to growing in *magis*. I encourage you to try them and see which ones are the most effective in experiencing the wholeheartedness you desire in the particular circumstance in your life that is causing you desolation and despondency. I recommend that you start your prayer time the same way that Ignatius recommends, by naming the grace that you desire. It might sound something like, "God, please give me the grace to choose *magis* in each moment of my day."

PATHS TO *MAGIS*

Growing in *magis* can happen both during, as well as outside of, personal prayer. The best way to start reflecting on *magis* during prayer is to use Ignatius' meditation on the Three Types of Persons. Just like Ellen, I recommend that you spend time in prayer imagining that God has entrusted three people with the difficult circumstance that you're struggling with right now in life. Imagine that the first person responds with lots of promises to help, but doesn't follow through. Pay close attention to how that response looks and sounds. Then, imagine the second person does lots of good things to try to help with the situation, but it just leads to more exhaustion. Using all of your senses in imaginative prayer, savor each detail of the meditation. Lastly, let the third person choose *the* good. What does that good look and sound like? In your particular circumstance, what word, prayer, or action would bring God the *greatest* glory? Share with God how that meditation gives you insight into how to respond differently to your difficult circumstance.

Another great way to grow in *magis* during personal prayer is to use a modified version of Ignatius' Examen. You don't have to be familiar with the Examen, or know its traditional five steps, in order to benefit from it. Instead, all you need to know is that the Examen is a simple and brief reflection on the previous hours of our day that can give us wonderful insight into how God has been present and how we are responding. The Examen can be simplified to spending a few minutes in prayer sharing with God your answers to a couple of reflection questions, such as, "When did I choose *the* good today?" and "When was I the most vulnerably intimate with God or others?" While Ignatius paused multiple times throughout the day to do this sort of reflection in order to grow in God-awareness and self-awareness, you might start with spending just a few minutes at the end of each day. Such daily reflection on our experiences of *magis* will help us be even more aware of and responsive to opportunities the next day.

A third way that you can grow in *magis* during personal prayer is to find a living person or a canonized saint who lived the *magis* you desire in circumstances very similar to yours. For example, Ellen read about Saint John of God, who lived in the sixteenth century, and learned what motivated him to care for the sick. She found a kindred spirit in John. She and John are both impulsive, compassionate, easily distracted, generous, and enjoy reading. Getting to know Saint John helped Ellen to better understand what *magis* looked like in his life of caring for those who were ill. It also gave her a deeper sense of companionship, which is a great source of wholeheartedness.

Like Ellen, you can find renewal through a person or a saint who models for you what *magis* looks like in your particular circumstance. If the circumstance in your life that is causing you to be half-hearted and exhausted is a person who constantly interrupts you and distracts you from what you need to be doing, then finding a kindred spirit in Saint Thérèse of Lisieux and learning what *magis* looked like in her experience could be wonderfully helpful. Or if your current desolate circumstance involves a broken relationship with your spouse, then becoming familiar with the gift of *magis* in the life of St. Rita of Cascia can help. Thankfully, the internet is filled with lists of patron saints and their stories, so finding kindred spirits is relatively easy.

The thing that has been the most helpful for me in growing in *magis* actually happens outside of personal prayer time and involves my phone. I frequently change the wallpaper on my smartphone to an image or phrase that reminds me to choose *magis* in each moment. That way, every time I look at my phone and use its many apps throughout the day, I'm reminded to choose vulnerable intimacy. In addition to that amazing reminder, I also use an app that allows God to randomly text me reminders to choose *magis*. I've found that those random texts often come at the most meaningful times.

I think the reason why *magis* increases our wholeheartedness is not necessarily because there's something deep within us that desires to "go for the gold," but because there is something deep within us that desires to be vulnerably intimate, authentic, and transparent in everything we do. Sure, we desire to feel successful, be a blessing to others, and make God proud of us, but not at the cost of being inauthentic or egotistical. We desire to be deeply real. Choosing to do *the* good, rather than just *a* good, can become a spiritual striving and purpose within our heart that is rooted in authenticity and fueled by the delight and glory that it brings to God.

CHAPTER FIVE

Wholeheartedness through Opposition

The Three Degrees of Humility

I was recently sitting on the balcony of the Donaghey Student Center at the University of Arkansas Little Rock watching my stepdaughter compete. She swims for a Division One university, and my wife and I were blessed with the opportunity to watch her and her teammates go up against UALR. If you've never been to a swim meet, the humid air at the pool is dripping with both the stench of chlorine and the excitement of athletes who have poured their hearts into the sport for years. Most of the swimmers, including Brianna, have been going to swim practice every morning and evening, six days a week, including many holidays, since they were in grade school. Knowing the complete dedication that the sport requires adds to the excitement of the competitions.

My favorite part of the fast-paced world of swim is the relay. It's inspiring to watch Brianna and her teammates encourage one another to do their very best. As I watched them swim against UALR, I found myself wondering—what are swimmers' greatest motivations? Do they push their mental and physical abilities in order to keep their athletic scholarships or to improve their individual swim times? Or is their extreme effort motivated by their desire to help their teammates or beat the competition? Rather than speculating, I asked Brianna what motivated her and her friends to swim the relays so passionately. She said that the two biggest sources of motivation are solidarity with her teammates and competition with her opponents. Interestingly, as I pondered those motivations, I realized that solidarity and opposition are two of the five sources of wholeheartedness that Ignatius teaches us in Week Two.

Ignatius' invitation for us to experience solidarity with Christ and opposition to the world are found in two meditations—the Two Standards and the Three Degrees of Humility. The similarities between the two meditations are striking, including Ignatius' focus on humility, poverty, and the world's contempt. Whereas in chapter three we looked closely at solidarity with Christ, which deepens our wholeheartedness through compassion, in this chapter we will look at the passion available to us through opposition to the world's values, views, and ways. It's important to note here that Ignatius uses the word "world" as a catchall for those values, views, and ways that are egotistical, rooted in the seven capital sins, and opposed to the Beatitudes, gifts of the Holy Spirit, and fruits of the Holy Spirit.

Ignatius learned during his time as a soldier that having something or someone to fight against can stir up tremendous zeal, effort, and sacrifice. He knew that opponents help us to create standards by which to live, teach us by their mistakes, and help us better understand our weaknesses. After his conversion, Ignatius incorporated that understanding in the *Spiritual Exercises* using the phrase *agere contra*, which means "acting against." He understood that to live a wholehearted life in solidarity with Christ requires that we choose to act against our false passions and the world's values, views, and ways. Since that seemed very logical to me, I mistakenly thought that *agere contra* was going to be an easy teaching to understand and put into practice, but instead I've found it very challenging.

As with most new things in my life, when I discovered Ignatius' teaching on *agere contra*, I poured my time, energy, and prayer into learning more about it. I wanted to truly understand what Ignatius meant by it and how to apply it to my life. What surprised and confused me as I began studying *agere contra* was that the majority of teachings and explanations I discovered in books and online grated against my spirit. As I read various articles and commentaries on Ignatius' teaching, the authors' words felt very egotistical and first-half-of-life, minimizing our opposition to the world to simply being perfectly obedient to the Church's teachings and shaming those who fall short.

The number of articles that subtly, and sometimes blatantly, took this approach to Ignatius' teaching shocked me. The articles sounded much more like today's political ads, filled with rancor, false passion, ego, and self-righteousness. I knew that finding authentic passion and wholeheartedness through opposition to the world's values and ways could not be degraded to the ego's desire to feel superior or to the self-righteousness of mechanically following rules as if we're merely automatons. I knew that Ignatius' encouragement for us to live *agere contra* had to be deeper, more intimate, and more relational, but I didn't yet know what that looked like theoretically or practically.

Sitting in eucharistic adoration one evening, I asked God to help me better understand what Ignatius was inviting us to experience through acting against the world. As I sat in quiet, the story of Jesus' condemnation of the scribes and Pharisees in chapter twenty-three of the Gospel of Matthew came to mind. Jesus said to them, "Woe to you, scribes and Pharisees, you hypocrites. You are like whitewashed tombs, which appear beautiful on the outside, but inside are full of dead men's bones and every kind of filth" (23:27). Reading that brief Scripture verse helped me to realize that, like most spiritual practices, *agere contra* can be done in an external and ego-based form where it is mostly just a mask covering our lack of interior conversion, or it can penetrate deeper and lead to authentic wholeheartedness. We can find examples of the former every day in the news.

Think about the numerous politicians and Church leaders who have publicly decried various ideologies and actions only to be exposed for engaging in the very acts and lifestyles they decried. There's the male state senator who, according to the Associated Press, routinely voted for anti-LGBTQ bills yet was arrested for soliciting sex from a 17-year-old boy. There is the televangelist who persistently preached on the importance of being good stewards of the money God entrusts to us, yet is being investigated by the Senate for misappropriating millions of dollars. These examples are not extraordinary; we see them in the news almost daily, and they remind us that, at various times in our lives, all of us fall into the trap of being nothing more than whitewashed tombs. In the Three Degrees of Humility, Ignatius challenges us to go beyond whitewashing and experience true interior conversion that sets us against the values of the world.

An authentically passionate and wholehearted life requires much more than external posturing; it requires an interior disposition of love marked with transparency, integrity, and peace. The famous NPR host, Krista Tippett, explains this beautifully in her book *Becoming Wise*, writing,

> A pattern of unintentional self-destruction [was] glorified in the twentieth century—to enrich on the outside, and impoverish within. Our kids [however] want us to finally get this right. They have injected the language of transparency and authenticity and integrity into our civic vocabulary....Behind [these words] I hear a wise refusal to disconnect what we know from who we are, what we believe from how we live and who we are to each other. Such words carry heartbreaking, holy longings for us to see ourselves in our wholeness—to make the move from intelligence to wisdom, from the inside.

In harmony with Tippett's observation, Ignatius' encouragement is for us to be in opposition to the world through a loving and interior vulnerability and integrity. What does *agere contra* look like for those of us who desire to cultivate that sort of interior conversion, authentic passion, and second-half-of-life relationship with God? How can our opposition to the world's values, views, and ways be more than simply an external, ego-driven whitewashing? My research and experience have shown me that there is one important thing to remember in order to let our opposition to the world be a source of authentic passion and wholehearted living—solidarity with the Divine. This is why Ignatius always linked the two together—solidarity with Christ and opposition to the world. When we disconnect them, it pulls our spiritual growth out of the context of relationship and the ego quickly turns it into an opportunity to feel better about ourselves behind a façade of being in control and looking down on others.

Our companionship with Christ better ensures that our opposition to the world is marked with the same humility, gentleness, and love that marked Jesus' opposition. Just as Brianna and her teammates don't hate the universities or competitors they swim against, you and I are not called to hate the world. While that might sound obvious, it's quite apparent that our culture frequently defines opposition as hatred. In fact, I believe that the spiritual, emotional, and intellectual immaturity of our society is most apparent and obvious in the fact that so few people seem to be able to disagree with one another without feeling the necessity to vilify and shame one another. Such hatred and animosity is not the type of opposition that Ignatius is advocating in the *Exercises*. Instead, authentic *agere contra* must be filled with love, peace, and hope. That is what the world witnessed when Saint John Paul II chose *agere contra* in 1999.

I remember the turn of the millennium well. I had just finished graduate school and was excited to move into the next stage of my life. However, there weren't many people who shared my excitement. Instead, the world was collectively growing in fear, anxiety, and despair. We were being told that Y2K—the year 2000—was going to bring with it a catastrophic collapse of the world's computer network that would lead to death and destruction. As most of the world fearfully stockpiled bottles of water and canned goods, there was one constant voice of hope—John Paul II. Rather than joining the voices of trepidation, he chose to stand in opposition to the world's message and proclaim hope. Rooted in love, peace, and joy, the pope's words helped shift our collective focus from the negative "what if" to the positive and eternal "what if" of Christ. Rather than promoting fear, he pointed out that the year 2000 was a threshold of hope. That is authentic *agere contra.*

Saint Francis of Assisi offers us another example of opposition to the world and solidarity with Christ. In the beginning of his ministry, Francis shared the world's fear of lepers. At that time, the primary way to avoid the disease of leprosy was to quarantine those who were infected and stay away from them. Francis found himself conflicted by that method because he understood the world's fear, but he also desired to imitate Christ, who did not quarantine and avoid lepers. In fact, in the gospels, Jesus actually *touched* lepers, rather than fearing them. Francis knew that choosing *agere contra*—opposition to the world's values, views, and ways—meant choosing to be in solidarity with Christ in how he treated lepers. This eventually led Francis to choose to not only be near them, but also kiss their wounds! That is authentic *agere contra*.

While those two examples of opposition to the world might seem sensational, there are simpler opportunities for you and me to live *agere contra*. For example, the world largely encourages us to hoard money out of fear that we will not have enough. As such, *agere contra* can be as simple as choosing to tithe even when it means losing some of our financial security. Or we can choose to be in opposition to the world's ways by peacefully walking away from gossip at work. Another expression of *agere contra* can be our willingness to dialogue with those who have different beliefs, listening to them, learning from them, and even falling in love with them. My point is that *agere contra* isn't about telling others that they're wrong, nor is it about hatred, division, and self-righteousness. It consists in looking for opportunities every day, including in the difficult situations in our lives, to join Christ in living and loving in ways that surpass what the world defines as sufficient and acceptable.

Opposition to the world is a deeper, more meaningful way of sharing in Christ's humility, poverty, gentleness, and love. The beautiful passion and wholeheartedness that can come from *agere contra* can be particularly helpful to us when we're feeling irrelevant or discouraged in our vocations or in the important decisions we've made in life, and when our solidarity with Christ needs to be taken to a deeper level in order to remain faithful to our commitment. That is what Joan experienced when she took a break from ministry in order to attend an eight-day silent retreat in Little Rock.

At the age of fifty-five, Joan found herself dissatisfied with her life as a teacher and made the decision to retire early in order to work at a soup kitchen in downtown Detroit. Her family thought she was crazy for giving up financial security as a tenured teacher for a life of financial uncertainty, and they frequently expressed their chagrin. Their opinion bothered Joan, but it didn't weigh on her in the beginning. However, after a year of working at the non-profit for a minuscule salary, her family's concerns felt more real, and her fear of financial instability grew. Without realizing it, the fear and second-guessing began to erode her love for the poor and her passion for serving them. She didn't recognize how profound the erosion was until one of her family members offered her a dream job with his company.

Her yearly salary at the soup kitchen was just over eighteen thousand dollars and was enough to pay rent on a simple apartment a few blocks from work, pay utilities, and put food on the table. There wasn't money left over each month for superfluous things like cable television or dining out. Those things would be a possibility again, however, if Joan accepted the job offer she received from the Fortune 500 Company her brother-in-law owned. He offered her a job teaching employees new strategies and assisting in their implementation. The challenge of the job, along with the travel and six-figure salary, were very appealing and caused Joan to question her work with the poor.

For a couple of months, her personal prayer time was marked with feeling irrelevant and discouraged in her ministry with the poor. The countless hours she spent serving the poor did not seem to help the profound urban decay happening in Detroit. She wondered if making a much larger salary, and donating a lot of it to the poor, could help even more of the destitute people living in Detroit than her work at the soup kitchen. It was out of those feelings and questions that Joan decided to go on a retreat to discern her future.

During her first spiritual direction session at the beginning of the retreat, Joan shared with me her desire for the retreat to bring clarity to her future. She felt confused about what God wanted her to do with her time, talents, and resources. She explained that many good Christian people were telling her to take the new job and use the extra money to help the less fortunate; they told her that such charity would be very pleasing to God and that God didn't want her to struggle financially. Their arguments were made even stronger by the fact that she didn't see much fruit coming from her current ministry with the poor. As she shared how she was feeling and what questions were most important to her, it became clear that her retreat would be marked with a lot of discernment.

Joan spent the first day simply settling into the retreat; she knew that detaching from the busyness and exhaustion of her life was the necessary first step in discerning. She slept a lot and tried to be more mindful of her movements, prayer, and eating. For her first few prayer times, I offered Joan some easy-to-enjoy Scripture verses, including Isaiah 55:1–2, that invited her to accept God's hospitality and to respond wholeheartedly to God's welcome. Just as you and I first welcome people into our homes before initiating deep conversations with them, it was important for Joan to be welcomed by God before settling into challenging conversations. Joan shared with me how relaxing it was to enjoy God's welcome and hospitality.

In the days that followed, I invited Joan to reflect on the Three Degrees of Humility. The meditation begins with a reminder that the fullness of humility and love is found in our choosing to imitate Christ, which will always be the opposite of what the world values. This becomes very clear in the meditation as Ignatius describes the three degrees, or levels, of humility as: 1) living the commandments and trying to avoid those things which would cut us off from God; 2) living the commandments as well as trying to follow God's will; and 3) living in such intimate union with Christ that we oppose the very things he opposed, namely the values and ways of the world.

The third and highest form of humility that Ignatius mentions requires such deep solidarity with Christ that we discover a surprising passion in opposing the very same worldly and egotistical views and ways that Christ opposed in the gospels. That is what Joan experienced as she used the meditation both during prayer and at various times outside of personal prayer. During prayer, I encouraged her to think of moments in her own life, as well as the lives of family members and friends, when she recognized each of the three levels of humility. I also invited her to reflect on the differences between Jesus' values and ways and the world's values and ways. Additionally, Joan tried to be open to recognizing opportunities to oppose the values, views, and ways of the world outside of her personal prayer time. These were simple experiences, such as choosing not to get on her cell phone and check email during her retreat, which would have simply been a distraction.

As the retreat unfolded, Joan meditated on additional Scripture verses that helped her to better understand the values and ways of Christ and how they're different than those of the world. For example, she spent several prayer times reflecting on the Beatitudes from the gospels of Matthew and Luke, and some of the "world's beatitudes" that I wrote years ago (and will share later in this chapter). She also spent time reflecting on Saint Paul's descriptions of the flesh versus the Spirit. As the retreat neared its end, I encouraged Joan to begin imaginatively viewing herself and her ministry in Detroit through the lens of Christ's values and then the world's values.

In one particularly relevant prayer time, Joan imagined Jesus with her at the soup kitchen and then Jesus with her in the new job that she was being offered. She realized that her deepest desire was to work *with* the poor, not *for* the poor. At one point in spiritual direction, Joan surprised herself by saying, "I feel like I was created to be with and to serve the poor." The soup kitchen offered her an opportunity to be with Christ and with the poor in a way that made no sense to the world, whereas the Fortune 500 job would take her away from daily relationship with the poor. Joan realized that, in order to wholeheartedly be who God created her to be, she had to choose solidarity with Christ in his love for the poor while being in opposition to how the world judges success and worth.

At the end of that particular prayer time, Joan wrote a letter to Jesus. She has given me permission to share part of the letter with you, which beautifully expresses her desire and passion to live an extraordinary life of opposition to what the world values, as well as what her misguided, but well-intentioned family, values.

> My Precious Jesus, I see you in the poor; I serve you in the poor; I love you in the poor. When I'm close to them, I feel close to you. When they are grateful for the food I offer them, I know you are grateful, too. My family does not understand any of this. I know they love me and they worry about me, but I hear you say to me, "fear is useless, faith is necessary." I have never been lacking food, clothing, or a dry and warm place to sleep. Thank you. I know that I'll never be Saint Francis or Saint Martin de Porres, whose radical love for the poor inspires me and confounds me. That is okay. But that doesn't mean I have to be wealthy, popular, or powerful either. I want to be me, working with those I love—the poor of Detroit. That is what excites my heart and I feel a strange satisfaction in knowing that I'm taking the "road less travelled" and not what the world would expect. Yes, I feel a satisfaction with our decision. Please give me the grace to find generosity and perseverance in that strange satisfaction.

When Joan returned to Detroit after the retreat, she turned down the job offer. She made a habit of beginning her prayer time each morning by reading Jesus' words in the Gospel of John, chapter sixteen, "I have told you this so that you might have peace in me. In the world you will have trouble, but take courage, I have conquered the world" (16:33). Then, after prayer and breakfast, she walks to the soup kitchen to be with the poor whom she loves, and she serves them with Christ, intentionally choosing to oppose the familial and societal voices telling her that what she does is not enough. It is more than enough; she is more than enough. That is authentic *agere contra.*

Like Joan, you and I sometimes draw motivation from both our ego and our faith—the world and Christ—which leaves us divided and, inevitably, feeling half-hearted, apathetic, and exhausted. We live with one foot in the world, desiring to be successful by its standards, and one foot in our faith, wanting to be with Christ. Instead, the Three Degrees of Humility meditation invites us to live in opposition to our egos and the world's values so that we can enter more deeply into the divine life. This is truly the whole purpose of the *Spiritual Exercises*—to completely restructure our life, values, and desires in solidarity with Christ and in opposition to the ego and the world. That restructuring doesn't happen all at once, but rather, it is a lifelong process of deepening our relationship with Christ and choosing *agere contra.*

Like Joan, Ignatius had opportunities to discern the world's view versus Christ's view, and to choose to fight against the former while being conformed to the latter. He wrote about one such opportunity in his autobiography, and it stands in contrast to a similar experience that happened to Ignatius years before his conversion.

As you might know, one of Ignatius' most prominent characteristics was his passion. Before his conversion, that passion was often directed by the world's values. For example, as a young man, it was reported that he angrily chased an enemy through town with his sword drawn, hoping to kill him. At that point in his life, Ignatius viewed his enemies the way the world does—as people to reject and destroy. However, that changed after his conversion.

Having spent time at school in Spain, Ignatius made the long journey to Paris to further his studies. While there, Ignatius had an opportunity to oppose the world's view of enemies when he got word that a man who had stolen money from him had fallen ill in Rouen. Rather than rejoicing at the news, Ignatius traveled to Rouen to see the man and to serve him. Ignatius chose to live Christ's teaching, "You have heard that it is said, 'You shall love your neighbor and hate your enemy.' But I say to you, love your enemies, and pray for those who persecute you" (Matthew 5:43–44a).

Jesus was challenging his disciples to oppose the world's view of enemies and embrace a new, more compassionate view, and Ignatius responded passionately and wholeheartedly to that challenge. In addition to walking barefoot, Ignatius chose to fast from food and water during the three-day journey as a way of spiritually preparing to serve his former enemy. Finally arriving in Rouen, he humbly and lovingly cared for the man who had robbed him. In the eyes of the world, Ignatius' actions are absurd; in Christ's eyes, they are passionately beautiful and wholehearted.

While our challenges may not be discerning work with the homeless or taking a shoeless journey to care for an enemy, they are still challenging. In the difficult circumstances in your life that are causing you to feel apathetic, half-hearted, and exhausted, how does the world generally respond? How does Christ respond? We can sum up the values, views, and ways of the world, the ego, and the flesh with words like division, alienation, disregard, selfishness, fear, disdain, anger, blame, shame, ignoring, power, prestige, manipulation, lies, facades, licentiousness, gossip, jealously, envy, greed, sloth, escapism, disowning, disobedience, recklessness, conceit, slander, ingratitude, callousness, and hate. By and large, the ways of the world are focused on helping us superficially feel better about ourselves regardless of lies that are perpetuated or the pain inflicted on others. That is very different from the ways and values of Christ.

The values and ways of Christ can be summarized as love, faith, hope, peace, solidarity, courage, generosity, magnanimity, service, selflessness, unity, humility, endurance, acceptance, openness, poverty, living on the fringe, kindness, warmth, joy, willingness, self-control, gentleness, mercy, meekness, sanctity, purity, and truth. His ways always reaffirm our authentic self-worth, hold others in love, bring unity, and radiate respect. Living as Jesus did requires us to look at every circumstance of our lives differently than the world does. Such a radical restructuring of how we see and understand life is the condition of discipleship that Jesus spoke about in the Gospel of Matthew, chapter sixteen, saying, "Whoever wishes to come after me must deny himself, take up his cross, and follow me. For whoever wishes to save his life will lose it, but whoever loses his life for my sake will find it" (16:24b–25). If you and I desire to grow in wholeheartedness, we must be willing to gently and lovingly oppose the ways of the world and embrace Jesus' values.

One of the most significant experiences of *agere contra* in my life has to do with pain and depression. Only recently did I realize that I have spent most of my life handling physical pain and waves of melancholy the way the world teaches—by disregarding them and by escapism. That hasn't worked out too well for me. At some level I must have known that the world sees health and happiness as supreme goods and promotes a very tangible prejudice against people who need pain medicine and against those who suffer from depression or other mental illnesses, because I spent years ignoring and running from my physical pain and melancholy.

As a priest, I never felt permission to be in pain or melancholic. That is not a criticism against the Church as much as it is an awareness of my lack of vulnerability and fear of love. I felt pressured to put on a happy face and be positive all the time. I know that I'm not the only one. A prominent priest in our diocese once promised his parishioners that no matter how he felt, he would always put on a smile at Mass. That breaks my heart! While I never said those words to my congregations, I did something similar—I tried to look happy when I was in public. I also unconsciously used hobbies to distract from the pain of degenerated discs in my back and neck and from the melancholy that is simply part of life. For example, I spent vacations and days off motorcycling all over the United States. Now, looking back, I can see that sometimes I rode to get away from things, not to get somewhere.

For years, I handled my pain and melancholy the way the world teaches—by stuffing my feelings and ignoring my pain. "Suck it up," was what the voice in my head often said, and so I did. But that is not how Jesus approached physical and emotional pain. Numerous times in the gospels we see Jesus being honest and open with his pain, including weeping at the death of his friend Lazarus (John 11), being angry at the moneychangers (Matthew 21), and being thirsty on the cross (John 19). Jesus acknowledged and named his suffering. I realized a couple of years ago that I needed to do the same. *Agere contra* for me means being more vulnerable and honest about how I am feeling. My wife has helped me to do that in meaningful ways.

Carmel has taught me that I don't have to be perfect and I don't always have to be happy. She has helped create space in my life for pain and melancholy. She holds that space for me through listening, gentleness, and love. I have grown comfortable saying to her, "I'm in a lot of pain right now." I could not have imagined saying those words ten years ago. Also, I have given myself permission to take pain medicine when physical pain begins impacting other aspects of my life. That, for me, is *agere contra*; it's a conscious choice to no longer keep parts of my life hidden or silent, but rather, to humbly model Christ's vulnerability and honesty.

What areas of your life are not yet aligned with the characteristics and values of Christ? When do you feel trapped by the values and reactions of the world? Learning *agere contra* through the Three Degrees of Humility can help us renew our passion and wholeheartedness. As with all of the avenues to wholeheartedness that we have looked at in this book, *agere contra* is not a one-and-done tool; it's not a quick fix. *Agere contra* is a lifestyle that you and I are invited to develop through consciously and repeatedly choosing to gently let go of the ways and values of the world and lovingly embrace the ways and values of Christ. Let's look now at some ways to cultivate that transformation.

PATHS TO *AGERE CONTRA*

Like Joan, you might enjoy spending time in prayer with the Three Degrees of Humility, reflecting on how the fullness of humility and love is found in choosing to imitate Christ, which is always in opposition to the things the world values. I recommend that you start the meditation by settling into the presence and love of God, which holds us in existence. Then, spend some time thinking about people you know who exemplify each of the three degrees, or levels, of humility—1) living the commandments and trying to avoid those things that would cut a person off from God, 2) living the commandments as well as trying to follow God's will, and 3) living in such intimate union with Christ that a person opposes the very things Jesus opposed, namely the values and ways of the world. End the meditation by sharing with God how each of those three people might handle the difficult circumstance or situation that currently leaves you feeling half-hearted.

Another great way to grow in *agere contra* is to spend time reflecting on the differences between Christ's view and the world's view and let them shape our day-to-day decisions. For example, use the Beatitudes in the Gospel of Matthew (5:3–12) and the Gospel of Luke (6:20–26) to learn more about Christ's values and ways of living and then compare them with the "world's beatitudes" that I wrote years ago.

- Happy are those who have a lot of new things.
- Happy are those who never lose anything.
- Happy are those who are led by their ego.
- Happy are those who overindulge in worldly things.

- Happy are the aggressive.
- Happy are those who work hard to appear valuable to others.
- Happy are those who are always right.
- Happy are those who are liked by everyone.

In addition to the Beatitudes, I recommend that you spend time reflecting on other Scripture passages that remind you of the differences between Christ's view and the world's view, including 1 Corinthians 2:12–14; Ephesians 6:10-17; Romans 12:2; 2 Timothy 3:1-9; John 16:33. As you meditate on these verses, savor the "strange satisfaction" that Joan wrote about on her retreat. There is, indeed, a strange satisfaction in *agere contra*. You might even take time to recall moments in your own life when you felt spiritual joy in choosing not to do what everyone else was doing. As you spend time reflecting on how *agere contra* can help you to live a more wholehearted life, be sure to ask God for the grace of tempering your opposition with love, gentleness, and humility.

CHAPTER SIX

Examples of Wholeheartedness

Can you think of an experience of wholeheartedness you've had that unintentionally flowed from one of the five sources that we savored in this book—companionship, our beginnings, compassion, *magis*, or opposition? Take a few deep breaths and be grateful for that experience. In this moment of pause, also be mindful of God's gratitude for your wholeheartedness. How does it feel to accept God's gratitude?

Being wholehearted does not require knowing and using the meditations I shared in the last five chapters, but it definitely helps. Those meditations give us an understanding and language that can assist us to more deeply savor our own experiences of wholeheartedness, as well as the wholeheartedness of extraordinary people like Viktor, Caleb, Natalie,

Jim, Thérèse, and Simone, whose lives are the centerpiece of this chapter. As you read their stories, I hope they remind you of the five specific sources of wholeheartedness that Ignatius teaches us in the *Exercises*. These men and women help us to see that the sources of wholeheartedness are not limited to five particular prayers in the *Exercises*; they are much more expansive than a meditation, a denomination, a religion, a culture, and a period of time. I also hope the following illustrations help you to see passion and wholeheartedness in your own story and inspire you to lean even more fully into your authentic self.

I was first introduced to Viktor Frankl during a psychology class in college. The class briefly studied some of the psychological principles that Frankl taught in his book *Man's Search for Meaning*. At the time, I didn't think much about his writing, but in graduate school I took the time to read the entire book and realized that Frankl put flesh and blood on my submarine image. He taught that a person can choose to go deeper into authentic passion and wholeheartedness even in a "sea" that he or she did not choose to traverse. That was Frankl's experience when, in 1944, the Nazis took him and his wife to the concentration camp at Auschwitz. Despite being held captive, he remained true to his training as a psychologist, reflecting on his own experience and on the experiences of those around him. As he did, Frankl discovered that there were prisoners who lost hope and those who did not. Even though they were all experiencing the same "sea" of life—they were all in the same place on the horizontal plane—they were at different depths of wholeheartedness, passion, and hope.

Noticing that difference among the prisoners helped Frankl realize that, "Everything can be taken from a man but one thing: the last of the human freedoms—to choose one's attitude in any given set of circumstances, to choose one's own way." That is the heart of this book—to learn from Saint Ignatius ways to spiritually and practically choose authentic passion and wholeheartedness in every circumstance of life, whether it's a circumstance that we painstakingly discerned or one that was thrust upon us. Deep within us, we know that such passion is necessary in life and for life. Most of us seem to instinctually know T.S. Eliot's truth that, "We must be still and still moving, into another intensity, for a further union, a deeper communion." Viktor Frankl lived that depth of wholeheartedness, as did the Old Testament character, Caleb.

In the book of Numbers, chapter thirteen, we read about God leading the Israelites to the Promised Land of Canaan. As they approached the outskirts, Moses sent a group of twelve men to reconnoiter the land to see if it was fertile and whether the people living there were strong or weak. When the men returned to Moses, all of them, except for Joshua and Caleb, had lost hope and were apathetic, fatigued, and resigned to failure because of the strength of the people whom they had encountered. Rather than being pulled into the prevailing apathy of the group, Caleb gave voice to the passion and wholeheartedness that God desired from the Israelites, saying, "We ought to go up and seize the land, for we can certainly prevail over it" (Numbers 13:30).

God blessed Caleb and Joshua for their faithfulness, passion, and wholeheartedness by allowing them to be the only two out of the twelve to enter into Canaan. Thousands of years before Ignatius wrote the Kingdom Exercise meditation, Caleb modeled for us the passion Ignatius tells us can come from remembering that God is companioning with us. Caleb and Joshua understood that they were taking over the land of Canaan *with* God, not just *for* God. When have you experienced renewed passion by remembering that you were serving with God and not just for God? How has God blessed you for your faithfulness, passion, and wholeheartedness?

Like Caleb, Natalie Diaz was not familiar with the *Spiritual Exercises*, yet, she courageously returned to her beginning when she realized that she was no longer living as authentically as she desired. Natalie is a Mohave Indian and a poet. Having played basketball on the reservation as a child, she left home to play at Old Dominion University and then in various women's leagues. Her life path not only took her physically further from the reservation, but also further from her spiritual and ancestral roots. At a pivotal point in her young adulthood, Natalie realized that her life was moving from sports to poetry; it was an existential shift that involved an interest in, and a desire to revive, her native language. This led her back to the beginning—to the Colorado River and mountains between California and Arizona that are home to the Mohave Indians.

Natalie now works with elders on the reservation, recording the stories, songs, and words that have been part of their heritage for generations. Additionally, she facilitates a weekly workshop for the youth in the tribe, most of whom have lost touch with their ancestral roots. They are brought together with elders and learn about the important history of their tribe. As those weekly workshops continue, many of the young Mohave will undoubtedly be just as impassioned and transformed by their encounter with their beginnings as Natalie. Returning to her roots has radically reshaped Natalie's life and led to renewed wholeheartedness and generous service. That is what happens when we take time to return to our beginning and savor our most authentic identity and experiences. Have you had a similar experience of returning to your roots? If so, how did you encounter God in that experience?

While returning to the beginning was an avenue of renewal and wholeheartedness for Natalie, it was compassion with Christ in the shared circumstance of suffering that rekindled Jim's passion. Jim Willig was ordained a priest for the Archdiocese of Cincinnati in 1977. While serving as pastor of Saints Peter and Paul Catholic Church, Jim was diagnosed with stage four renal cell cancer. It was devastating news for him and his congregation. Through the help of one of his parishioners, Jim began to write about his experience with cancer and how it helped connect him more intimately and compassionately with Christ.

Like the shared condition that we read about in the Two Standards meditation, Jim's suffering helped bond him compassionately to Jesus. He shared about his deepening intimacy with Christ, as well as the rekindling of wholeheartedness that he experienced through his cancer treatment, writing,

> Upon entering the school of suffering, I learned that [my] former way of prayer was not adequate. It didn't take long for me to understand that I was being invit-

> ed to relate to the Lord at a deeper level, where I had not yet developed that more intimate way of communicating with him….In those true moments of peace, I can honestly say it matters little to me whether I suffer much or live a long or short life. All that matters is that I remain one with Jesus. (*Lessons from the School of Suffering*, pp. 29, 34)

Those words became particularly comforting to Jim's family and friends when cancer eventually claimed his life at the age of fifty. All the way to the end, Jim discovered and intensified his wholeheartedness through a deep sense of remaining "one with Jesus" in his suffering. Can you think of a time when you were able to compassionately connect with Christ in your suffering? What was that compassion like and how did you respond to it?

Saint Thérèse the Little Flower was also a student of suffering. Like Jim, she grew in wholeheartedness through what she suffered, as well as through *magis*. Born in 1873 in France, Thérèse experienced her share of suffering throughout her life, from being a sickly infant to dying of tuberculosis at the age of twenty-four. Despite it all, she persevered with a desire to serve God. When her health would not allow her to serve God in the ways she considered big, like doing missionary work overseas, Thérèse chose to start doing small things with great love. She decided to choose *the* good in each circumstance of her life, even the seemingly mundane ones. She describes this desire in her autobiography, *The Story of a Soul*, writing,

> I will seek out a means of getting to Heaven by a little way—very short and very straight, a little way that is wholly new....I ought to seek the companionship of those Sisters towards whom I feel a natural aversion, and try to be their Good Samaritan. A word or a smile is often enough to put fresh life in a despondent soul. And yet it is not merely in the hope of giving consolation that I try to be kind. If it were, I know that I should soon be discouraged, for well-intentioned words are often totally misunderstood. Consequently...I try to act solely to please Our Lord.

Without intending to live a particular aspect of the *Spiritual Exercises*, Thérèse's simple spirituality helps us to understand what *magis* can look like in everyday life. It's about following Jesus' invitation to go the extra mile in how we love through our words, actions, and prayers. It's about choosing *the* most vulnerable and intimate response in the ordinary circumstances of life, even being kind to annoying nuns. Take a moment to think of a time when you chose to do something small with great love. How did that experience affect your spirit?

Like the nuns Saint Thérèse described, some people consider Sister Simone Campbell to be a nuisance; yet she is a wonderful example of the passion and wholeheartedness that can come from being in loving opposition to the world. If you're not familiar with her work, Sister Simone wears a lot of proverbial hats, including being a Catholic nun, a lawyer, a lobbyist, and a practitioner of Zen. Through her work as executive director of NETWORK, a lobbying organization, Sister Simone has set herself in opposition to the values, views, and ways of our society in the hope of serving the most vulnerable among us.

Her life of *agere contra* stands in stark contrast to the vicious and malicious opposition that we commonly see in the politics of Washington. Hers is an opposition grounded in love. Her conversations about her opponents are respectful and kind. For example, in talking about Paul Ryan, who has been an opponent of Sister Simone's progressive social opinions, she said, "Paul Ryan is doing his part. And I'm doing my part. And we spend our lives annoying each other kind of. I mean, he enjoys sparring with me and I enjoy sparring with him. So even though we've been working on opposite sides in a way, my intersection has affected him and he's affected me. And I think we're better for it" (*On Being*, NPR interview). I doubt that Sister Simone wakes up each morning and consciously chooses to live *agere contra*, yet her spiritual journey has led her to the truth that Ignatius teaches us—that loving opposition to the world can be a source of passion and wholeheartedness. Have you ever annoyed someone by simply living the values of Christ? What did that *agere contra* feel like for you?

Now that we know about the five sources of authentic passion and wholeheartedness, we can witness the examples of their power and meaning in our life and in the lives of the people around us. And it's really important for us to take the time to savor those examples and experiences, letting them remind us of the ways God deepens our generosity, willingness, availability, magnanimity, and love. Who are the people in your life who model the wholeheartedness that you desire?

What do those five sources of passion look like in their life? How have you already experienced and lived one or more of those five sources of wholeheartedness in various areas of your life? As we take time to answer those questions, we might discover that many "submarines," including our own, have gone to depths that we had not even realized.

CONCLUSION

The desire you and I have for wholeheartedness is deeply important. In fact, it's a desire that is vital for the health and future of our world. While that might sound overdramatic to some people, it's a simple and practical truth for those of us who recognize the division, hatred, selfishness, and apathy that has infiltrated our world through rampant half-heartedness and hard-heartedness. Every day, you and I hear far more stories about people who have callously acted in selfishness than those who have generously acted in *magis*. Rather than being discouraged, however, we can choose to be agents of change and transformation in our families, communities, and world by putting our wholeheartedness into practice through the lessons and spiritual tools Ignatius offers to us in the *Spiritual Exercises.*

Our desire for wholeheartedness, then, must be about more than just ourselves, and this book must be more than just another self-help read. Our desire for wholeheartedness is about becoming the wisdom figures our world desperately needs; it's about becoming men and women who are growing past false passions that are rooted in egos and ideologies, and becoming people who T.S. Eliot wrote can "be still and still moving" and who have chosen to be explorers "into another intensity, for a further union, a deeper communion." So, it's truly no small thing that you and I desire to live wholehearted and authentically passionate lives of availability, love, acceptance, and magnanimity, even in the most difficult, as well as seemingly insignificant, circumstances in our lives.

Frequently, I have to go back to the five lessons about wholeheartedness that Ignatius teaches in Week Two and intentionally choose the companionship, beginning, compassion, *magis*, and opposition that allow me to be the unique, particular image of Christ that God created me to be for the world today. And for as many times as I make that conscious choice, there are twice as many times that I selfishly or apathetically don't. I recognize that wholeheartedness—since it's ultimately rooted in relationship—is a lifelong process that requires continual work. Despite the effort it entails, I'm very grateful that God gives me opportunities every day to push through the gray ashes of difficult moments so as to discover the burning ember of an authentically wholehearted life. I can promise you, it's always there—a burning ember beneath the surface of the difficult circumstances in our lives, much like the hot ember I found buried beneath the ash in a thurible many years ago.

It was after a holy day celebration, and I had taken off my vestments and was straightening up the church, when I saw that the thurible had not yet been cleaned. We had used incense for the celebration and, glancing into the metal bowl hanging on a gold chain, I could see the gray ashes from the charcoal. I knew that I needed to make sure the charcoal was fully extinguished before I dumped it in the trash, so I pushed my finger into the cool pile of ash. While my brain was still calculating the risk involved in that action, I pushed my finger deepwardly, through the ashes, and hit the red-hot ember beneath, burning myself. That ember reminds me to this day that, even though we sometimes think there is nothing left to rekindle in our lives, or that we must resign ourselves to living in desolation, apathy, or exhaustion, there is certainly an ember available if we choose to go deeper.

As you choose to act on the wholeheartedness you desire, let me offer some encouragements and practical tips. A couple of them I mentioned earlier in the book, and a few of them are new. All of them are ways that I use to keep my desire for wholeheartedness on the forefront of my heart and mind so that I can be intentional in choosing to go deeper. I will not share them in any particular order, but as you try each of them, you might find that some are more beneficial and fruitful for you than others.

The most obvious suggestion is to keep using the meditations in this book during your personal prayer time. They are not one-time prayer moments; we must go back to the five reflections in Week Two over and over, going deeper into relationship with Christ and letting ourselves be transformed from the inside out. I find myself returning to those five meditations several times a month, especially when I realize I missed opportunities for wholeheartedness. Also, if you're in spiritual direction, be sure to share with your director when you feel the Spirit prompting you to return to one or more of those meditations, as well as share what new insights and healings you experience through them.

As I mentioned in chapter four, my cell phone is one of my favorite tools for growing in wholeheartedness, or any virtue for that matter. Every couple of weeks, I change the wallpaper to a word or image that reminds me of the topic of conversation that Jesus and I are having in personal prayer. Those words and images remind me multiple times each day to be more authentic, vulnerable, and wholehearted. When I find that a particular word or image no longer captures my attention when I turn on my phone, I change it to a new one. Whereas twenty years ago, we would have used written reminders in order to develop good habits, we are blessed to have a digital reminder in our hands that we see countless times throughout the day. And, since our phones are now "smart," they offer apps that can remind us randomly throughout the day to choose wholeheartedness.

Another important tool for choosing the wholeheartedness we desire is the Examen. It's the spiritual practice that I mentioned at the end of chapter four. Ignatius practiced the Examen multiple times throughout the day, and people say that by the time he died he was doing the Examen almost constantly. It formally entails five steps—thanking God, praying for the light of God's perspective, reviewing the day so as to be aware of God and how we're responding to God's grace, asking for forgiveness for any lack of response to God's grace, and making a choice to respond differently in the future. However, many who practice the Examen simplify it to reviewing part of our day with God so as to know how we can respond more wholeheartedly in the future. It's a spiritual practice that doesn't have to take long, yet it definitely helps us to be more conscious and intentional in our spiritual and personal growth.

Reading is another important tool for me. I consciously

choose to read books by people whom I respect as wholehearted individuals and whose books encourage me to live more wholeheartedly and authentically, including authors like Richard Rohr, James Martin, Maureen Conroy, Wilkie Au, Joseph Tetlow, Mark E. Thibodeaux, Stephen Binz, Ronald Rolheiser, Brené Brown, and Thomas Merton. For the most part, I try to read spiritual books that reflect a topic very similar to the one I'm having with God in personal prayer. In other words, if I'm spending days or weeks praying with God about my desire to grow in *magis*, then I'll generally look for a book or article to read outside of prayer that also has to do with *magis*. I have found that this creates a really meaningful continuity, which reinforces the virtue I desire.

Authentic wholeheartedness cannot exist apart from vulnerability and intimacy. Therefore, if we want to grow in wholeheartedness, it will inevitably entail seizing opportunities to be open, honest, exposed, and real, especially with people who, in the words of Brené Brown, have earned the right to hear our stories. Vulnerability is not easy for me; I have to consciously choose at various moments to share with people my pain, struggles, and hopes. Other than God, my wife has been the single biggest influence in my willingness to be vulnerable. Her unconditional acceptance of who I am has taught me that I don't have to hustle for worth or hide in fear. Until we learn that lesson, we cannot be as wholehearted as we desire.

Lastly, mentors are indispensable to our growth. I am grateful that my spiritual journey has been marked with, and shaped by, the companionship of close friends, especially Cindy Shaw, Tom Jakobs, and a wonderful spiritual director,

Fr. Mark. During a very formative time in my spiritual growth, the three of them modeled for me a wholeheartedness that included deep love, acceptance, generosity, openness, and vulnerability. Then, when I went through the painful transition of leaving the priesthood, their wholeheartedness became even more meaningful to me; it was a warm embrace of acceptance and love that stood in contrast to the cold shoulder I got from people who told me that I was a failure and disappointment. Each of us needs men and women who mentor for us the wholeheartedness that we desire. Who are those people in your life? How much time do you make to be with them, enjoying their stories and being encouraged by their choices?

One of the mentors who has blessed my life, Brené Brown, in her book *Daring Greatly*, explains that "there are many tenants of Wholeheartedness, but at its very core is vulnerability and worthiness: facing uncertainty, exposure, and emotional risks, and knowing that I am enough" (pg. 38). I hope the meditations in this book help you face the uncertainty and difficult circumstances in your life with acceptance and generosity; I hope they help you to take emotional risks with deep vulnerability and intimacy; and, I hope that the meditations allow God to remind you that you are, in fact, enough. That is the wholeheartedness I desire; that is the wholeheartedness you desire.